BATTLE OF BRITAIN

RAF AIRFIELDS
Ground Attacks

James Robertshaw

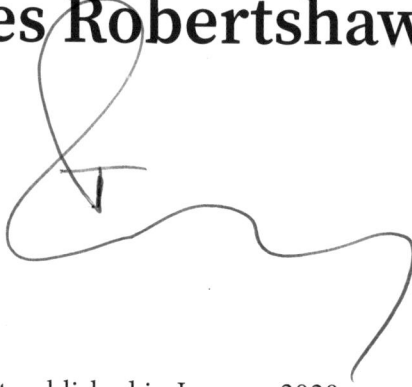

First published in January 2020
Revised and updated September 2020
Copyright © James Robertshaw

ISBN 978-1-9161841-3-8

Contents

Preface

This work is a study of how Britain was prepared, in 1940, against a German invasion and the attacks that took place by the Luftwaffe on our airfields and the defences taken against an invasion.

The period covered is from July to October 1940* and describes the air defences and the attacks the Luftwaffe carried out trying to smash the RAF in a prelude to a German invasion of the British Isles.

Britain faced a real threat of invasion following the defeat at Dunkirk Operation Dynamo), plans had been drawn up by the Germans (Operation Sea Lion), the Germans had to first destroy the RAF on the ground before invasion.

Britain did not have long to re-organise its defences and this book highlights preparations, and what attacks the Germans made.

The Battle **for** Britain (not **of** Britain)…..We needed every bit of courage and planning we could muster.

Donations from the sale of these books will be made to the RAF Benevolent Fund and Help 4 Homeless Veterans.

---

* Official Battle of Britain dates 10th July to 31st October 1940.

Chapter 1
Britain's Position June 1940

Britain had declared War on Germany in October 1939 following Poland being invaded by German forces and the subsequent invasion by Germany of Czechoslovakia, Norway, Denmark and annexation of Austria. The British had sent an expeditionary force of 300,000 into Belgium and the Germans had subsequently invaded Holland, Belgium, Luxembourg and defeated the Allies in France. A mass evacuation was made of the BEF (British Expeditionary Force) at Dunkirk. Operation Dynamo evacuated nearly 350,000 British, French and Belgian soldiers from the Dunkirk Beaches. (338,226 from 26th May to 4th June).

Britain was next for Invasion. Adolph Hitler drew up plans for invasion under *Operation Sea Lion* from the ports in Northern France. Britain had to prepare its home defences against invasion. Britain was vulnerable.

Operation Dynamo - over 850 small craft were used to ferry troops to larger ships, they were attacked constantly by the Luftwaffe, but 192,226 British 110,000 French and 22,698 Dutch and Belgian troops were rescued from the 26th May to the 4th June using the beaches and the mole.

RAF Squadrons in France 1940
Prior to Dunkirk AASF (Advanced Air Striking Force)

Air Vice Marshal Patrick Playfair, AOC 1 Group, Bomber Command/AASF

Air Marshal Arthur Barratt, AOC British Air Forces in France and Air Vice-Marshal Patrick Playfair, AOC Advanced Air Striking Force

Squadrons in France in 1940

The RAF supported Operation Dynamo from 11 Group which became part of the Forward Operating Bases (FOB) as well as the airfields left in France which were evacuated, the RAF protected the BEF evacuation.

These squadrons were sent to France or operated in England to assist the BEF and also the evacuations from Dunkirk. The RAF had very poor command and control in France before Dunkirk.

Airfields used in France were: Dieppe, Reims, Vassincourt, d'Etain-Rouvres, Plivot, Bétheniville. Orleans, Vraux.

AIRCRAFT		SQUADRONS - QUANTITY & SQN. NUMBER	PLANES / SQN	LOSSES
Lysander	5	2, 4, 13, 16, 26	18	118
Blenheim Bomber	12	21, 70, 79, 81, 82, 83, 86, 88, 107, 110, 114, 139	15	135
Hawker Hurricane	6	1, 73, 218, 226, 242, 501	12	77
Hurricane		Group 11 support	380	105
Spitfire	10	Group 11 support	72	29
Fairey Battle	10	12, 15, 40, 88, 103, 105, 142, 15, 218, 226	15	67
Whitley Bomber	9	71, 72, 74, 75, 76, 77, 78, 102, 218	15	70
		Totals:	1,359	601

RAF No1 Sqn Hawker Hurricane at Vassincourt

Evacuating RAF personnel from Brest - Operation Ariel

RAF 139 Sqn Bristol Blenheim

RAF 142 Sqn Fairey Battle

The House of Commons passed the following pieces of Legislation:

1. Emergency Powers (Defence) Act 1930 and 1940.
2. Treachery Act 1930.
3. National Armed Services Act 1940.
4. Defence of the Realm Land Acquisition Act 1916 - improved.
5. Compulsory Armed Forces Conscription, 1.5 million men.
6. Lord Beaverbrook appointed Minister for Aircraft Production May 1940 - took Standard Motors, etc. more Spitfires and Hurricanes, home production.
7. Air Raid Protection Act 1937 revised.
8. Allied Forces Act 1940, allow other countries to keep armies in UK.
9. Camps Act 1939 - Evacuation of urban residents, children and elderly.
10. Military Training Act 1939 and National Service Act 1941.

Anti Invasion Operations and Plans.
(To bolster the defences of Britain)

1. Home Guard Units formed May 1940; Local Defence Volunteers.

2. Political Warfare Department set up; Evacuation of children.

3. Deception and Propaganda Department set up, posters to inform the public self defence, loose talk, etc.

4. Planned Resistance Units set up (Auxiliary Units - Secret Army), www.staybehind.com. Coleshill HQ - Faringdon - Swindon area - Brigadier Hamilton Bailey.

5. Formation of the Women's ATS (Auxiliary Territorial Service) to assist armed forces on non armed roles.

6. Anti Invasion Plans set up - Stop Lines - Taunton, GCHQ, Tyne, Conquest Lines. Removal of street signs, church bells banned.

7. Programme of Field Fortification, Pill Boxes, Anti Tank ditches.

8. Coastal Defence Programme - Maunsell Forts (Rough Sands, Sunk Head, Knock John, Nore, Red Sands, Shivering Sands, Tongue Sands) Coastal Crust areas.

9. Air Raid Shelters built, Air Wardens appointed, Gas Masks issued to all households and Airfield Protection programmes. Civil Defence units set up.

10. Food production and use of land, Women's Land Army. Rationing.

11. Special Operation Executive formation Hugh Dalton and Major General Gubbins (separate book: www.dday-wardiaries.co.uk)

THE HOME GUARD 1939-1945 The Home Guard: Photograph (L) contrasting a 1940 Local Defence Volunteer with a 1944 Home Guard.

Maunsell Forts

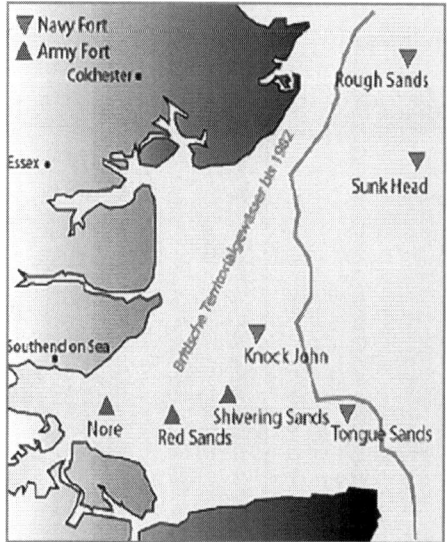

Navy and Army Forts 1940

Pickett-Hamilton Pillbox

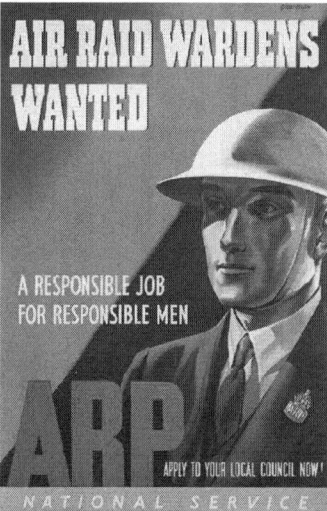

*Air Raid Wardens Wanted
poster*

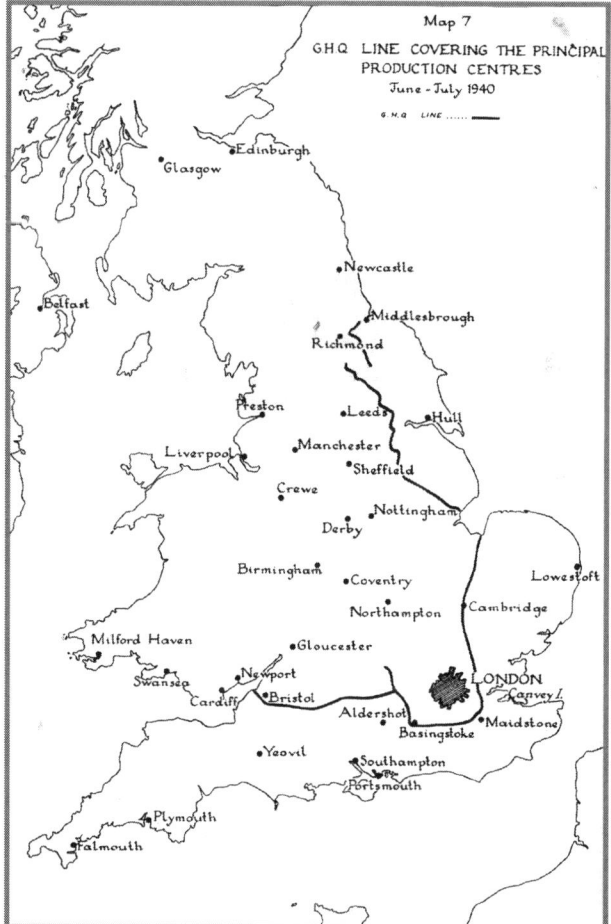

Defence Stop Lines

Anti-Invasion Operations to Bolster British Defences

Anderson Air Raid Shelter

Secret Army Bunker

Civil Defence Training

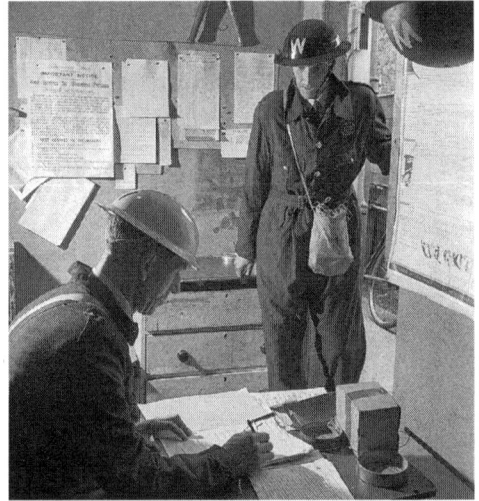
Air Raid Precautions (ARP) Wardens

Local Defence Volunteers (LDV)

Homemade Shelter

LDV - Home Guard Units used to protect public assets and infrastructure from attack.

Local Defence Volunteers: 'Old Contemptibles'

Blitz West End Air Shelter

Anderson allotment shelter

Underground Station shelter - used until 14.9.40

Posters encouraging self-reliance

Weekly Ration Allowance

Bacon–4oz; Sugar–8oz; Tea–2oz; Meat–1 shilling; Cheese–2oz; Milk–3 pints; Eggs–1/week; Preserves–1 lb every 2 months; Butter–2oz; Margarine–4oz; Lard–4oz; Sweets–12ozs every 4 weeks.

Rationing did not end until 1958.

Evacuation - Operation Pied Piper

From the Camps Act 1939 to move 1.5 million children and vulnerable people into the countryside from urban areas. Under the Women's Voluntary Service (WVS) – 17,000 officers were appointed to find billets, schools, etc. for those to be evacuated.

Children Evacuees (1939)

Children Evacuees

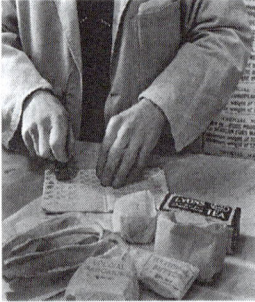

Food Rationing

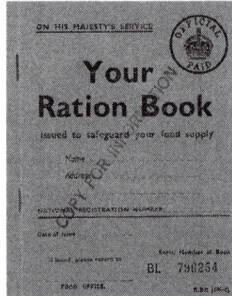

Child's Ration Book

Evacuation of children to the country

Chapter 2
Maps of Britain's Air Defence

The War Cabinet reorganised the Air Defences of Britain and the early warning systems from Chain Home Radar and the Royal Observer Corps.

Group 11 was on the front line and squadrons were sent from Groups 10, 12 and 13 to help defend Britain.

There was a lot of inter-fluency during the Battle of Britain replacing squadrons for rest, etc.

Military Structure Reorganisation & Commanders

A RAF Fighter Command

B RAF Coastal Command & Royal Naval Air Stations

C Chain Home Radar

D Royal Observer Corps

E Army - Royal Artillery and Coastal Defence

F Army - Royal Engineers.

G Royal Navy - Atlantic Convoy Protection and Escorts and Port Defences (Not covered in this book,)

RAF Structure other than Front Line

No 1 Group - (Air Combat HQ) Intelligence, Planning, Recon - RAF High Wycombe, Coningsby, Lossiemouth, Waddington.

No 2 Group - (Air Combat Support) Look after assets, equipment etc, RAF Benson, Brize Norton, Odiham and Northolt.

No 22 Group - (Training) Supply qualified personnel - RAF Cranwell, Cosford, Walton, Linton, Shawbury, St Athan, Morgan and Valley.

No 38 Group - (Air Combat Service Support) Engineering & Maintenance - supply and maintain aircraft for operations. RAF High Wycombe and Wittering.

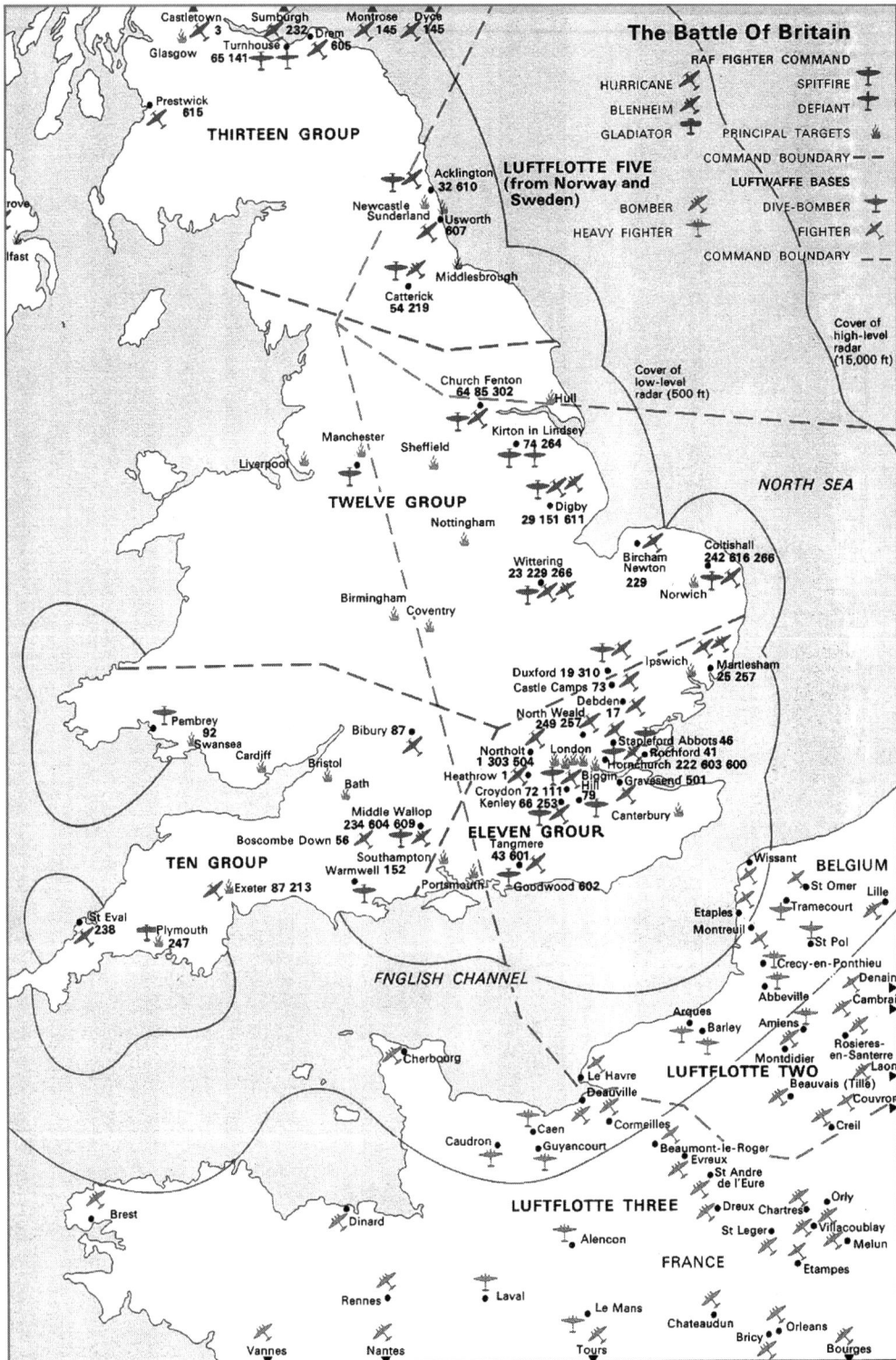

The Battle Of Britain

RAF FIGHTER COMMAND

HURRICANE   SPITFIRE
BLENHEIM   DEFIANT
GLADIATOR   PRINCIPAL TARGETS
COMMAND BOUNDARY — — —

LUFTWAFFE BASES
BOMBER   DIVE-BOMBER
HEAVY FIGHTER   FIGHTER
COMMAND BOUNDARY — — —

Castletown   Sumburgh   Montrose 145   Dyce 145
Turnhouse   232   Drem 605
Glasgow   65 141
Prestwick 615

THIRTEEN GROUP

Acklington 32 610

LUFTFLOTTE FIVE (from Norway and Sweden)

Newcastle
Sunderland   Usworth 607

Middlesbrough

Catterick 54 219

Church Fenton 64 85 302   Hull

Kirton in Lindsey 74 264

Manchester   Sheffield
Liverpool

TWELVE GROUP

Nottingham

Digby 29 151 611

Wittering 23 229 266

Bircham Newton 229

Coltishall 242 616 266

Norwich

Birmingham   Coventry

Duxford 19 310
Castle Camps 73
Debden 17
North Weald 249 257

Ipswich   Martlesham 25 257

Pembrey 92
Swansea
Cardiff
Bristol
Bath

Bibury 87

Northolt 1 303 504   London
Heathrow 1
Croydon 72 111
Kenley 66 253

Stapleford Abbots 46
Rochford 41
Hornchurch 222 603 600
Biggin Hill 79
Gravesend 501
Canterbury

Middle Wallop 234 604 609
Boscombe Down 56

ELEVEN GROUP

Tangmere 43 601

Southampton
Warmwell 152

Portsmouth   Goodwood 602

TEN GROUP

Exeter 87 213
St Eval 238
Plymouth 247

NORTH SEA

Cover of high-level radar (15,000 ft)
Cover of low-level radar (500 ft)

FNGLISH CHANNEL

Cherbourg

Wissant
St Omer   Lille
Tramecourt
Etaples   St Pol
Montreuil
Crecy-en-Ponthieu
Denain
Abbeville   Cambrai
Arques   Amiens
Barley
Rosieres-en-Santerre
Montdidier   Laon
Le Havre   **LUFTFLOTTE TWO**
Deauville   Beauvais (Tille)
Cormeilles   Couvron
Caen   Creil
Caudron   Guyancourt
Beaumont-le-Roger
Evreux
St Andre de l'Eure
Dreux Chartres   Orly

BELGIUM

LUFTFLOTTE THREE

Brest
Dinard
Alencon
St Leger   Villacoublay
Melun

FRANCE

Etampes

Rennes   Laval
Le Mans
Chateaudun   Orleans
Bricy   Bourges
Vannes   Nantes   Tours

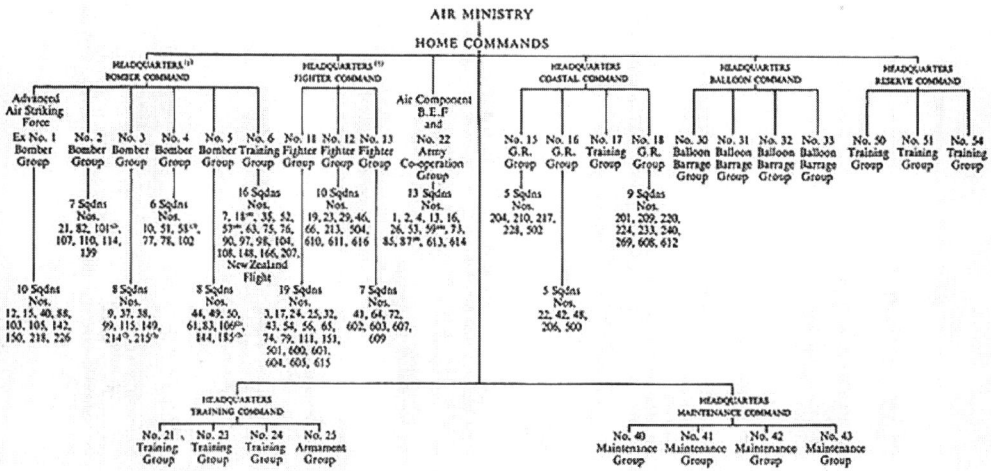

AIR MINISTRY

HOME COMMANDS

| HEADQUARTERS (1) BOMBER COMMAND | HEADQUARTERS (1) FIGHTER COMMAND | HEADQUARTERS COASTAL COMMAND | HEADQUARTERS BALLOON COMMAND | HEADQUARTERS RESERVE COMMAND |

Advanced Air Striking Force

Ex No. 1 Bomber Group | No. 2 Bomber Group | No. 3 Bomber Group | No. 4 Bomber Group | No. 5 Bomber Group | No. 6 Training Group | No. 11 Fighter Group | No. 12 Fighter Group | No. 13 Fighter Group | No. 22 Army Co-operation Group | Air Component B.E.F and | No. 15 G.R. Group | No. 16 G.R. Group | No. 17 Training Group | No. 18 G.R. Group | No. 30 Balloon Barrage Group | No. 31 Balloon Barrage Group | No. 32 Balloon Barrage Group | No. 33 Balloon Barrage Group | No. 50 Training Group | No. 51 Training Group | No. 54 Training Group

7 Sqdns Nos. 21, 82, 101(1), 107, 110, 114, 139

6 Sqdns Nos. 10, 51, 58(1), 77, 78, 102

16 Sqdns Nos. 7, 18(2), 35, 52, 53(1), 63, 75, 76, 90, 97, 98, 104, 108, 148, 166, 207, New Zealand Flight

10 Sqdns Nos. 19, 23, 29, 46, 66, 213, 504, 610, 611, 616

13 Sqdns Nos. 1, 2, 4, 13, 16, 26, 53, 59(2), 73, 85, 87(2), 613, 614

5 Sqdns Nos. 204, 210, 217, 228, 502

9 Sqdns Nos. 201, 209, 220, 224, 233, 240, 269, 608, 612

10 Sqdns Nos. 12, 15, 40, 88, 103, 105, 142, 150, 218, 226

8 Sqdns Nos. 9, 37, 38, 99, 115, 149, 214(1), 215(1)

8 Sqdns Nos. 44, 49, 50, 61, 83, 106(2), 144, 185(2)

19 Sqdns Nos. 3, 17, 24, 25, 32, 43, 54, 56, 65, 74, 79, 111, 151, 501, 600, 601, 604, 605, 615

7 Sqdns Nos. 41, 64, 72, 602, 603, 607, 609

5 Sqdns Nos. 22, 42, 48, 206, 500

| HEADQUARTERS TRAINING COMMAND | | | | HEADQUARTERS MAINTENANCE COMMAND |

No. 21 Training Group | No. 23 Training Group | No. 24 Training Group | No. 25 Armament Group | No. 40 Maintenance Group | No. 41 Maintenance Group | No. 42 Maintenance Group | No. 43 Maintenance Group

Squadron

Flight — Flight

Section — Section — Section — Section

Blue one
Green one
Yellow one
Red one

Blue three   Blue two
Green three   Green two
Yellow three   Yellow two
Red three   Red two

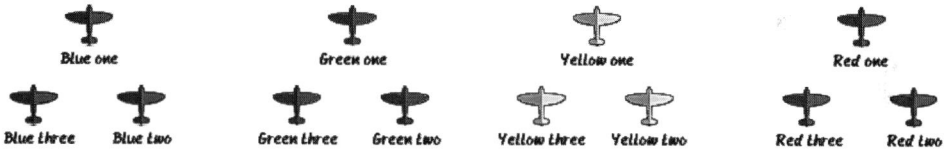

Fighter Aircraft	10 Group	11 Group	12 Group	13 Group	Total Squadrons
Spitfires	3	15	2	nil	20
Hurricanes	5	25	3	5	38

Structure of Groups, Wings and Squadrons

Every squadron had 2 flights A and B, looked after by a Flight Lieutenant; then 2 sections of 9 aircraft. Bomber squadrons had 2 flights of 7-8 aircraft per section and Ground staff were spit into sections. Each Flight had 1 Flying Officer in charge and 8 pilots. Total - 24 men and 2 sections per flight.

Summary of RAF Squadrons Used

(Location to end Sept. 1940 – moved because of attacks)

SQUADRON	AIRCRAFT	CODE	AIRFIELD/S			
			JULY	AUG	SEPT	OCT
№ 1	Hurricane	JX	Northolt	Northolt	Wittering	North Weald
№ 1 RCAF	Hurricane	YO	Croydon	Croydon	Northolt	North Weald
№ 3	Hurricane	QO	Wick	Wick	Turnhouse	Manstone
№ 17	Hurricane	YB	Debden	Debden	Debden	Debden
№ 19	Spitfire	QV	Fowlmere	Fowlmere	Fowlmere	Fowlmere
№ 23	Blenheim	YP	Collyweston	Collyweston	North Weald	Lympne
№ 25	Blenheim	ZK	Martlesham	Martlesham	Martlesham	Middle Wallop
№ 26	Lysander		West Malling	West Malling	West Malling	West Malling
№ 29	Blenheim	RO	Debden	Digby	Digby	Debden
№ 32	Hurricane	GZ	Biggin Hill	Biggin Hill	Acklington	Acklington
№ 41	Spitfire	EB	Catterick	Catterick	Hornchurch	Hornchurch
№ 43	Hurricane	FT	Tangmere	Tangmere	Usworth	Biggin Hill
№ 46	Hurricane	PO	Digby	Digby	Stapleford	North Weald
№ 54	Spitfire	KL	Rochford	Hornchurch,	Catterick	Rochford
№ 56	Hurricane	US	North Weald	Boscombe D	North Weald	North Weald
№ 64	Spitfire	SH	Kenley	Kenley	Ringwald	Kenley
№ 65	Spitfire	YT	Hornchurch	Hornchurch	Turnhouse	Hornchurch
№ 66	Spitfire	LZ	Coltishall	Coltishall	Gravesend	Kenley
№ 72	Spitfire	RN	Biggin Hill	Acklington	Acklington	Biggin Hill
№ 73	Hurricane	TP	Church Fenton	Church Fenton	Debden	Debden
№ 74	Spitfire	ZP	Hornchurch	Hornchurch	Wittering	Biggin Hill
№ 79	Hurricane	NV	Biggin Hill	Acklington	Pembrey	Biggin Hill
№ 85	Hurricane	VY	Martlesham	Martlesham	Church Fenton	Church Fenton
№ 87	Hurricane	LK	Exeter	Exeter	Bibury	Bibury
№ 92	Spitfire	QJ	Pembrey	Pembrey	Biggin Hill	Biggin Hill
№ 111	Hurricane		Croydon	Croydon	Drem	Drem
№ 141	Defiant	TW	Biggin Hill	Prestwick	Biggin Hill	Biggin Hill
№ 145	Hurricane	SO	Tangmere	Westhampnett	Dyce	Tangmere
№ 151	Hurricane	DZ	North Weald	North Weald	Digby	North Weald
№ 152	Spitfire	UM	Acklington	Warmwell	Warmwell	Middle Wallop
№ 213	Hurricane	AK	Exeter	Exeter	Tangmere	Tangmere
№ 219	Blenheim	FK	Catterick	Catterick	Catterick	Acklington
№ 222	Spitfire	ZD	Kirton	Kirton	Hornchurch	Hornchurch
№ 229	Hurricane	HB	Wittering	Wittering	Northolt	Northolt
№ 232	Hurricane	EF	Drem	Sumburgh	Sumburgh	Sumburgh
№ 234	Spitfire	AZ	St Eval	St Eval	St Eval	Middle Wallop
№ 235	Blenheim	LA	Manston	Filton	Filton	Filton

SQUADRON	AIRCRAFT	CODE	AIRFIELD/S			
			JULY	AUG	SEPT	OCT
№ 236	Blenheim	FA	Thorney Island	St Eval	St Eval	St Eval
№ 238	Hurricane	VK	Middle Wallop	Middle Wallop	Middle Wallop	Middle Wallop
№ 242	Hurricane	LE	Coltishall	Coltishall	Duxford	Biggin Hill
№ 245	Hurricane	DR	Turnhouse	Aldstigton	Aldstigton	Hawkinge
№ 247	Gladiator	HP	Roborough	Roborough	Roborough	Roborough
№ 248	Blenheim	WR	Dyce	Dyce	Dyce	Dyce
№ 249	Spitfire	GN	Leconfield	Church Fenton	North Weald	North Weald
№ 253	Hurricane	SW	Turnhouse	Turnhouse	Kenley	Kenley
№ 257	Hurricane	DT	Hendon	Northolt	Martlesham	North Weald
№ 263	Whirlwind	HE	Grangemouth	Grangemouth	Drem	Drem
№ 264	Defiant	PS	Duxford	Kirton	Northolt	Fowlmere
№ 266	Spitfire	UO	Wittering	Eastchurch	Wittering	Hornchurch
№ 302	Hurricane	WX	Westhampnett	Oxford	Oxford	Westhampnett
№ 303 *	Hurricane	RF	Northolt	Northolt	Northolt	Northolt
№ 306	Hurricane		Church Fenton	Church Fenton	Church Fenton	Church Fenton
№ 310	Hurricane	NN	Duxford	Duxford	Duxford	Duxford
№ 312	Hurricane	DU	Church Fenton	Church Fenton	Church Fenton	Church Fenton
№ 350	Spitfire		Croydon	Croydon	Croydon	Kenley
№ 501	Hurricane	SD	Croydon	Gravesend	Kenley	Biggin Hill
№ 504	Hurricane	TM	Castletown	Castletown	Hendon	Hendon
№ 600	Blenheim	BQ	Manston	Manston	Hornchurch	Hornchurch
№ 601	Hurricane	UF	Tangmere	Tangmere	Acklington	Croydon
№ 602	Spitfire	LO	Drem	Drem	Westhampnett	Westhampnett
№ 603	Spitfire	XT	Turnhouse	Dyce	Hornchurch	Hornchurch
№ 604	Blenheim	NG	Northolt	Middle Wallop	Middle Wallop	Middle Wallop
№ 605	Hurricane	UP	Drem	Drem	Croydon	Croydon
№ 607	Hurricane	AF	Usworth	Usworth	Tangmere	Tangmere
№ 609	Spitfire	PR	Middle Wallop	Middle Wallop	Middle Wallop	Middle Wallop
№ 610	Spitfire	DW	Gravesend	Biggin Hill	Biggin Hill	Biggin Hill
№ 611	Spitfire	FY	Digby	Digby	Digby	Digby
№ 614	Hurricane		Kenley	Kenley	Kenley	Kenley
№ 615	Hurricane	KW	Kenley	Kenley	Kenley	Kenley
№ 616	Spitfire	YQ	Church Fenton	Leconfield	Kenley	Kenley

* Note: Sq303–Polish squadron famous for highest number of kills.

Bristol Blenheim

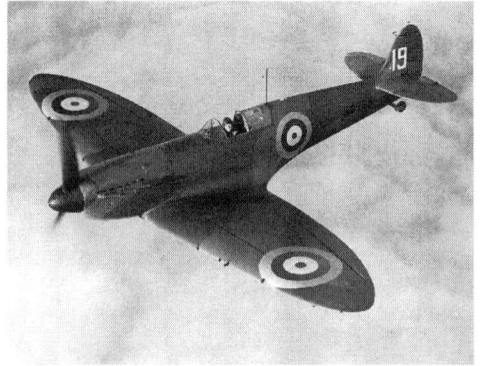

Supermarine Spitfire

Defiant Aircraft

Hawker Hunter Hurricane

Avro Anson

Short Sunderland Flying Boat

A - Fighter Command, Bentley Priory

*Air Chief Marshal,
Sir Hugh Dowding*

*(Above) Fighter
Command, Bentley
Piory, Stanmore*

*(Left) Rudloe Manor RAF
Box - planning room*

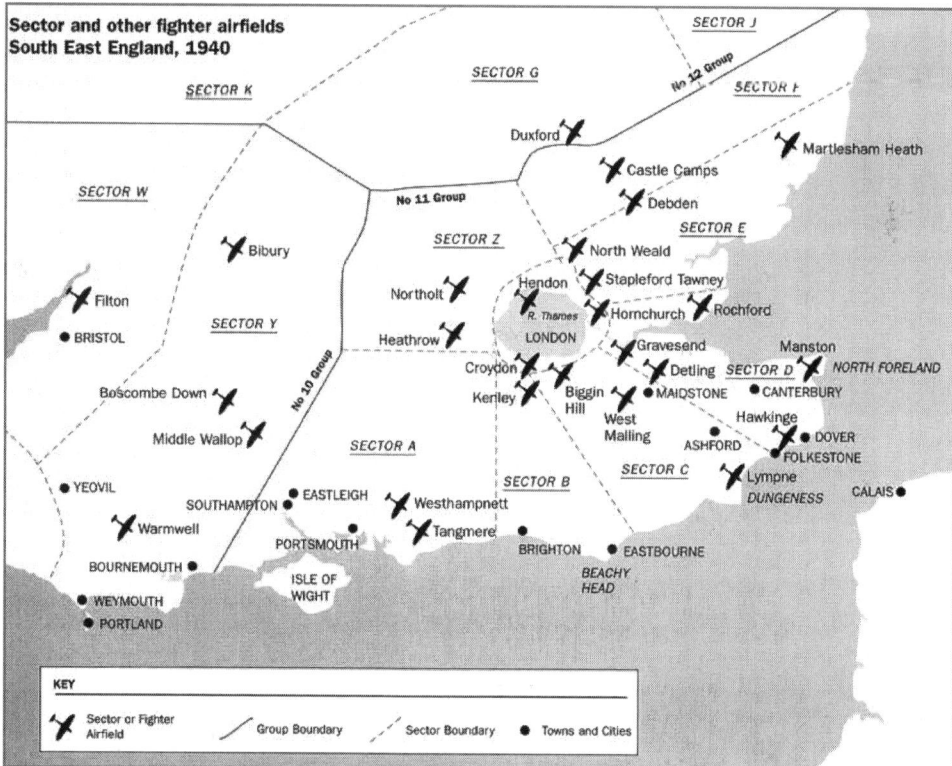

**Sector and other fighter airfields
South East England, 1940**

SECTOR J

SECTOR G

SECTOR K

No 12 Group

SECTOR F

Duxford

SECTOR W

No 11 Group

Castle Camps

Martlesham Heath

Debden

SECTOR Z

SECTOR E

Bibury

North Weald

Filton

Northolt

Hendon

Stapleford Tawney

● BRISTOL

SECTOR Y

Heathrow

R. Thames

LONDON

Hornchurch

Rochford

No 10 Group

Croydon

Gravesend

Manston

Boscombe Down

Kenley

Detling

SECTOR D

NORTH FORELAND

Biggin
Hill

MAIDSTONE

● CANTERBURY

Middle Wallop

SECTOR A

West
Malling

Hawkinge

● YEOVIL

SECTOR B

ASHFORD

● DOVER

FOLKESTONE

SOUTHAMPTON ● ● EASTLEIGH

Westhampnett

SECTOR C

Lympne

● Warmwell

Tangmere

PORTSMOUTH ●

BRIGHTON

● EASTBOURNE

DUNGENESS

CALAIS ●

BOURNEMOUTH ●

ISLE OF
WIGHT

BEACHY
HEAD

● WEYMOUTH

● PORTLAND

KEY

| Sector or Fighter Airfield | Group Boundary | Sector Boundary | ● Towns and Cities |

SE England - Sector Airfields 1940

No 10 Group HQ
Rudloe Manor, Box, Wiltshire

RAF Pembrey - W.C. Hutchinson - № 92 Spitfires (moved)

RAF Halton; RAF Finmere; RAF Little Horwood

RAF Aston Down 5OTU Spitfires & Blenheims

RAF Filton G Capt Hanmer № 87 Hurricane S.L. Lovell-Greg, № 236 Blenheim 8AACU

RAF Sutton Bridge 6OTU Hurricanes & Spitfires

RAF Hawarden 7OTU Hurricanes & Spitfires

RAF Pucklechurch - Relief Airfield, Balloon units № 935

Air Vice Marshal
Sir Christopher Brand

Barrage Balloon unit (County of Glamorgan)

RAF (RNAS) St Eval Coastal Command G Capt Croke № 234 Spitfires - S.L. O'Brien № 247 Gladiators F. Lt Chater.

RAF (RNAS) Roborough - № 247 - Gladiators Plymouth

RAF Bibury - № 87 - Hurricane

RAF Upper Heyford (France) Blenheims, № 70, 79, 81, 82, 83. To France - Whitley Bombers 71, 218, 72, 74, 75, 76, 78 (Bicester, Abingdon, Harwell, Benson, Boscombe)

RAF Middle Wallop - W.Com. Roberts - № 238 - Hurricane S.L. Fenton, № 604 Blenheims S.L. Anderson, № 609 Spitfires S.L. Darley, № 152 Spitfires S.L. Devitt, 249 (moved to Hornchurch)

RAF Boscombe Down-№35 -Halifax, №56 -Hurricane (moved to N.Weald) №109 -Ansons

RAF Colerne (satellite to Boscombe) night fighter training. № 238 Operational Conversion.

RAF Exeter - № 213 Hurricane, S.L. McGregor, - № 601 Hurricane (moved to Tangmere), № 87 (moved from Filton)

RAF Warmwell (Dorset) - № 152 - Spitfires (moved to Middle Wallop)

RAF Little Rissington

RAF Pengam Moors (Cardiff) - № 614 and № 43 - Hurricane (moved to Tangmere)

RAF Pembroke - № 10 RAAF, № 203, 209, 210 and 240.

RAF Swansea -part № 92 -Spitfires.

RAF Carew - Cheriton - № 48 Beauforts, № 75 Wellingtons № 217 - Ansons, № 14 Balloons

RAF Angle № 32 Hurricane (Biggin Hill) № 70 Army Coop

RAF Bibury № 87 Hurricane

RAF Llandow № 38 Maintenance Unit other bases in South Wales Not operating until 1941.

RAF Box (Wiltshire)- Rudloe Manor, Central Ammo Depot, Provost Training Centre.

RAF Brize Norton - № 2, 15, 16 Air Training

RAF Bicester - № 3, 17 Air Training & №1 Camouflage

RAF Benson № 1 Air Training

RAF Harwell - Bombers № 25, 105, 107, 148, 215, 276, 295, 570

RAF Broadwell

RAF Fairford (Not built until 1943)

A lot of front Squadrons were moved to Group 11 to defend the South East - Front Line Squadrons Group 10 Spitfires № 92, 152 and 234 Hurricanes № 87, 152, 213, 238. № 92 and 87 covered Wales.

*Air Marshal
Sir Keith Park*

No 11 Group HQ - Hillingdon House, Uxbridge

Air Vice Marshal Sir Keith Park

This group would bear most of the German Luftwaffe onslaught and therefore had the most fighter units and Coastal Command Units, as this was the closest to the coast of France.

RAF Stormy Down Training and also RAF Desford - Tiger Moths 92 Squadron. Training units were mainly in Oxfordshire.

Squadrons on the Front Line

Spitfires Total 15; Nos 41, 54, 64, 65, 66, 72, 74, 92, 222, 266, 350, 602, 603, 609, 610.

Hurricanes Total 25; Nos 1, 1(CAN), 3, 17, 25, 32, 43, 46, 56, 79, 85, 111, 145, 151, 229, 245, 249, 253, 257, 302, 303, 605, 607, 609, 616, 614.

Hillingdon House

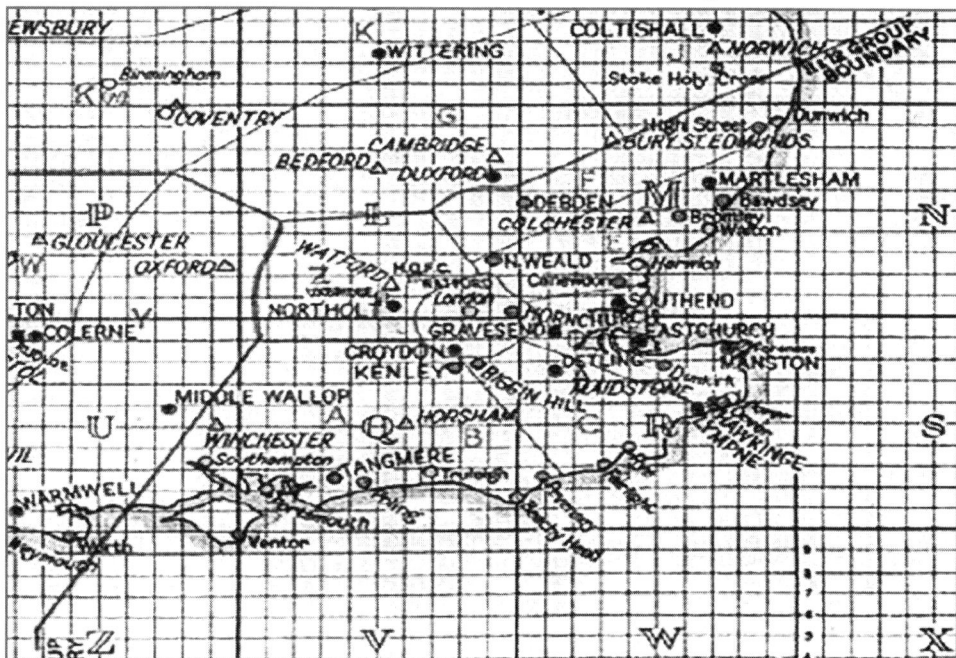

Number 11 Group

RAF Debden (Sector E) Wing Commander J.L.F. Fuller-Good: №17 - Hurricane; S.L Williams №85 - Hurricane; S/L Peter Townsend №29 - Blenheim; №257 - Hurricane; S.L Harkness; RAF Rochford (sector D) subsidiary to Hornchurch №54 - Spitfire; RAF North Weald (Sector E) W.Com. Victor Beamish: №56 - Hurricane; S/L Manton №151 - Hurricane; S/L Teddy Donaldson №57 ; RAF Castle Camps, RAF Church Fenton (Sector E) Nos 73 and 249 - Hurricane (Eagle Squadrons); RAF Martlesham Heath (Sector E) №25 S/L L.K.McEwan, Blenheim, Anti Aircraft 99th & 302nd HAA; RAF Stapleford Abbots-Tawney (Sector E) subsidiary №46 - Hurricane, №242, Special SOE Squadron №419 - Whitley Bombers.

RAF Hornchurch (Sector D) W.Com. Cecil Bouchier: №41 - Spitfire, №54 - Spitfire, S/L Leathart №65 - Spitfire S/L Holland, №74 - Spitfire, S/L Francis White, №92 - Spitfire, №266 - Spitfire, S/L Wilkinson №603 - Spitfire, №222 - Spitfire; RAF Gravesend (Sector D) №66 S/L A.T.Smith, №501 (Night Fighters) S/L Harry Hogan, №601 - Hurricane; RAF Manstone (Sector D) №3 - Hurricane (Attacked); RAF Woodcote - Maintenance, №600 S/L Dave Clark - Blenheim; RAF Dover Swingfield (Sector D) Nos 119 and 819 Naval Air Squadron.

RAF Biggin Hill (Sector C) W.Com. Richard Grice: №32 - Hurricane; S/L Worrall, №610 - Spitfire; S/L John Ellis, №501 - Hurricane; S/L Hogan №79 - Hurricane, №72 - Spitfire; №141 S/L Richardson - Defiants; RAF Red Hill Penshort (Sector C) №15 Training School, №16 - Lysander, №219 - Blenheim; RAF Croydon (Sector B) №111 S/L John Thompson - Hurricane, №350 - Spitfire (Belgian), №605 - Hurricane; RAF Lympne (Sector C) №s 2, 16, 18 - Blenheim, №s 23, 53 - Blenheim, №59 Blenheim; RAF West Malling (Sector C) №26 - Lysander, №141-Defiant.

RAF Kenley (Sector B) W.Com. Tom Prickman: №615 - Hurricane; S/L Kayll №64 - Spitfire; L Macdonell №1(RCAF) - Hurricane; №l McNab №253 - Hurricane №616 - Spitfire, №66 Spitfire; RAF Hawkinge (Sector B) №245 - Hurricane.

RAF Northolt (Sector Z) G.Capt Vincent: №1 RAF - Hurricane; L. Pemberton, №303 (Polish) - Hurricane; S/L Z. Henneberg №600 - Blenheim; L.D. Clark №111 - Hurricane; L. Thompson, №229 - Hurricane; RAF Heathrow (Sector Z) №1; RAF Heston (Sector Z)- damaged №1 PRU moved; RAF Hendon (Sector Z) RAF Transport Squadrons №601 & №604 & №257 S/L Bayne all moved; RAF Uxbridge (Sector Z)- Bentley Priory - Stanmore HQ Royal Observer Corps - Air Commodore Masterman.

RAF Tangmere (SectorA) W.Com. Jack Poret: №43 -Hurricane; L Tubby Badger №145 - Hurricane; L Peel, № 601 - Hurricane; L Hon Edward Ward №607 - Hurricane, №614 - Hurricane; RAF Shoreham (Sector A)- Station Com. Wing Com. George Chambelaine - subsidiary Tangmere: №224 - Lysander, №422 - Hurricane; RAF Goodwood Westhampnett (Sector A): №81, №602 - Spitfire, №302 (Polish) - Hurricane; No1493 Fighter Gunnery, №83 Air Support, №121 Airfield, №402 Air Stores Park; RAF Box Yapton (Sector A) №8 Service Uni, №23 (moved to Lympne), №131 (Polish) - Hurricane.

No 12 Group Watnall, Nottingham
Air Vice Marshal Trafford Leigh Mallory

*Vice Marshal Trafford
Leigh Mallory*

Watnall Fighter Command

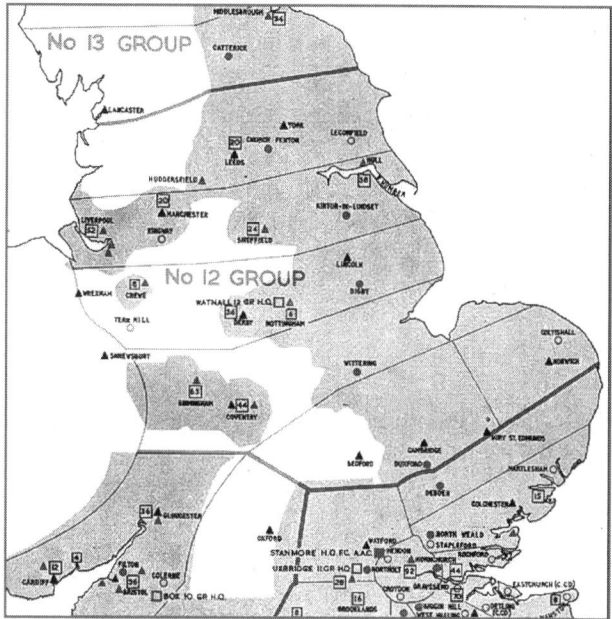

RAF 12 Group

<u>RAF Church Fenton</u> - G.Capt C.F. Horsley: Sq №73, S/L More - Hurricane (moved to Debden Castle Camp); Sq №249, S/L Eric King - Hurricane (moved to North Weald); Sq №616, S/L Marcus Robinson - Spitfire (moved to Kenley); Sq №312 (Polish), S/L Jack Satchell - Hurricane.

<u>RAF Kirton in Lindsey</u> - W.Com. S Hardy: Sq №222 S/L Johnnie Hill (moved to Hornchurch) - Spitfire; Sq №264, S/L Des Garvin (moved to Hornchurch) - Defiant.

<u>RAF Digby</u> - W.Com. Ian Parker: Sq №46, S/L MacLachlan (moved to Stapleford) - Hurricane: Sq №29, S/L S.Widdows - Blenheim; Sq №611, S/L James McComb (operated from Duxford) - Spitfire.

<u>RAF Coltishall</u> - W.Com W Beisiegel: Sq №242 S/L Douglas Bader - Hurricane; Sq №66 S/L Rupert Leigh (moved to Kenley)-Spitfire.

<u>RAF Wittering</u> - W.Com Harry Broadhurst:-Sq №229 S/L H.Maguire (moved to Northolt) - Hurricane; Sq №23 S/L G. Heycock (moved to Lympne - Middle Wallop - RNAS) - Blenheim.

<u>RAF Collyweston</u> (satellite to Wittering) - №5 Air Training Squadron.

<u>RAF Duxford</u> - W.Com A. Woodhall: Sq №19 S/L Pinkham (operated from Fowlmere satellite station) - Spitfire; Sq №310 (Czech) S/L Douglas Blackwood (operated from 18th Aug) - Hurricane.

<u>RAF Fowlmere</u> (satellite to Duxford): Sq №2 and №16 - Lysander; №15 - Fairey Battle; №21 - Blenheim; Sq №154 and №174 - Spitfires (1942); Sq №411 and №422 (CAN) - Hurricane; Sq №655 Austin 1941; Sq №264 moved.

RAF Tern Hill (satellite to Digby): Sq №24 Maintenance Unit, № 611 (moved to Digby), №46 (moved).

RAF Leconfield: Sq №166 - Whitley Bomber, (moved to Abingdon); Sq №234 Blenheim (moved to Church Fenton).

Front Line Units available, as most Spitfire and Hurricane squadrons had been moved to Group 11. Spitfires - Sq №19; Hurricanes - Sq №242, №310, №312 and №611.

RAF Groups 10 to 13

No 13 Group Blakelaw Estate, Newcastle upon Tyne Air Vice Marshal Richard Saul

Air Vice Marshal Richard Saul   *RAF 13 Group Blakelaw, Kenton Bar Bunker*

RAF Catterick - W.Com G.Carter: Sq №219 S/L J. Little (moved to Redhill) - Blenheim; Sq №41 S/L H.R. Hood (moved to Hornchurch) - Spitfire.

RAF Usworth - W.Com Brian Thomas: Sq №607 S/L James Vick (moved to Tangmere) - Hurricane; Sq №72 S/L A. Collins (moved to Biggin Hill, Croydon operated from satellite station) - Spitfire; Sq №79 S/L Hayworth (moved to Biggin Hill) - Hurricane.

RAF Wick W.Com Geoffrey Ambler: Sq №3 S/L S. Godden (moved to Kenley)-Hurricane; Sq №504 S/L John Sample (moved to Northolt) - Hurricane; Sq №232 S/L M. Stephens - Hurricane.

RAF Castletown (satellite to Wick): Sq №504 - Hurricane; №808 - FAA Fulmer.

RAF Dyce - G.Capt F. Crerar: Sq №603 (moved to Hornchurch) - Spitfire.

RAF Turnhouse (satellite to Dyce): W.Com Duke of Hamilton & Brandon: Sq №605 S/L Walter Churchill (moved to Croydon) - Hurricane; Sq №602 S/L Sandy Johnstone (moved to Westhampnett) - Spitfire; Sq №253 S/L Tom Gleave (moved to Kenley) - Hurricane; Sq №141 (moved to West Malling) -Defiant; Sq №245 S/L (moved to Aldergrove) - Hurricane; Sq №81 Hurricane.

RAF Acklington: Sq №79 (moved), Sq №7 Training, Sq №32 (moved), Sq №72 & Sq №152 (moved), Sq №409 - Beaufighter; RAF Leconfield: Sq №616 moved to Kenley, №245 moved.

RAF Drem: Sq №145 (moved), Sq №232 - Hurricane, Sq №263 - Hurricane.

RAF Grangemouth: Sq №58 Training Unit, Sq №141 (moved) - Blenheim; Sq №606 (moved) - Spitfire.

RAF Sunburgh (Shetlands): Sq №42 - Hurricane; Sq №144 - Torpedo Torbeau, Sq №404 - Beaufighter; RAF Montrose (Flying Training) Sq №603 - moved to Hornchurch.

RAF North Coates (transferred to Coastal Command): Sq №22, №235, №236, 248 - Blenheim.

RAF Skitten (transferred to Coastal Command): Sq №48, №86, №14, №172, №179, №217, №232, №260 - Blenheim.

RAF Stornoway (transferred to Coastal Command): Sq №48, №612 - Avro Anson, Sq №213 Signals; RAF Acklington Sq №s72 & 152 - Spitfire (moved).

RAF Sullom Voe (transferred to Coastal Command): Sq №201, №240 Saro London; Sq №204, №210 - Sunderland.

RAF Luce Bay (West Freugh): Sq №10 Air Training, Sq №4 Air Gunnery School.

Total Spitfires - nil, moved to Group 11; Total Hurricanes - 5, Sq №81, №232, №245, №263, №504 to protect Group 13.

Coastal Command HQ, Northwood
Air Chief Marshal Sir Frederick Bowhill

Coastal Command HQ, Eastbury Park

Sir Frederick Bowhill

UK Coastal Command Groups

*Princess Alice, (right) with
Lady Dorothy Bowhill*

*RAF Coastal Command,
Operations Room*

Groups 15 & 19 Air Commodore R.G.Parry DSO

RAF Aldergrove: Sq №503 Avro Anson, Whitley Bomber.

RAF Hutton Park: Sq №48 Avro Anson.

RAF Mountbatten (Plymouth): Sq №10 №204 Sunderland Flying Boat.

RAF Pembroke Docks: Sq №10 Sunderland, Sq № 209, 210 and 228 Sunderland Flying Boat.

RNAS St Eval: Sq №217 Beaufort, Sq №236 Blenheim.

RNAF St Merryn (HMS Vulture): - various.

RAF Warmwell: Sq №219 Avro Anson.

RNAS Culdrose (HMS Seahawk): opened 1947.

RNAS Yeolvilton (HMS Heron): RNAS Sq №750 and №794.

RAF Roborough (HMS Drake Plymouth): various later; №691 Hurricane (1943).

RAF Stormy Down (Wales) Sq №92 moved.

Group 16 Air Commodore R.L.G.Marix DSO

RAF Bircham Newton: Sq №42 Vickers Wilderbeest, №206 Avro Anson.

RAF (RNAS) Rochford (Sector E): Blenheim, - №w Southend Airport.

RAF Gravesend (Sector D): Sq №66 and №501 (Night Fighter), №601 Hurricane.

RAF (RNAS) Eastchurch (Sector D): №266 Blenheim (attacked).

RAF (RNAS) Detling (Sector D): Sq №500 Anson; Sq №53 and 235 Blenheim (at-tacked); №1 Coastal Artillery Group Anti Aircraft №4 Lysanders.

RNAS Lee on Solent (HMS Daedalus): №3 Baracuda Maintenance and №1 Avenger Maintenance, many RNAS Units.

RAF Thorney Island: School of General Reconnaissance, Sq №22 Vickers Wilde-beest, Sq №48 Avro Anson, Sq №59 Blenheim.

Group 17 Air Commodore T.E.B. Howe

RAF Calshot: Seaplane Training.

RAF Gosport (HMS Sultan): Group Capt Grenfell - №2 Anti Aircraft Co-Operation Squadron; Torpedo Training Unit; Torpedo Sq №s460. 461, 462, 463; Flight Spotters Sq №s420, 421, 422, 423; Air Stores Sq №401.

Campbelltown (HMS Landrail): RNAS Machrihrimanish; RNAS 780-1853.

Christchurch (HMS Raven): - Radio Station, moved to Eastleigh Town Hall, airfield transferred to USAF Crail (HMS Jackdaw); Sq №27 Training Depot RNAS 711-846.

Dunibristle (HMS Merlin): RNAS 700-1842.

Skaebrae (HMS Terne); RNAS Arbroath (HMS Condor) attacked Oct 1940 - Sq №65, №662 and RNAS 751-1730.

Group 18 Air Vice Marshal C.D. Breese

RAF Dyce: Sq №248 and №254 - Blenheim; Sq №612 Avro Anson.

RNAS Hatston (Kirkwall) (HMS Sparrow Hawk): Sq №254, Sq №200; Skulas, Sword-fish and Avengers Sq №700 NAS to №899.

RAF Invergordon: Sq №209 Stranraer, Sq №240 Saro London.

RAF Leuchans: Sq №224 and 233 Hudsons, Sq № 320 Dutch Avro Anson.

RAF Montrose: Sq № 268 Astro Anson.

RAF Sullom Vae: Sq №201 and 204 Sunder-land Flying Boat.

RAF Thornaby: Sq №220 and 608 Avro Anson.

RNAS Ford (Yapton) (HMS Perigrin): attacked 18th August 1940 - (Group 16).

RNAS Yeovilton Ground Crew

Coastal Command Insignia

Royal Air Force Marine Branch Air Sea Rescue 1940 Group Captain L.G. Le B Croke

The service was organised by Vice Admiral Bertram Russell and Air Vice Marshal Keith Park as a joint service, as 20% of aircraft shot down landed in the sea and had to be rescued. The service was updated following the Battle of Britain in 1941. There were various bases – RAF Bridlington on the Yorkshire Coast and RAF Bridport in Dorset and some RNAS stations. There were many other centres later in 1940 attached to Coastal Command bases. High Speed launches were used – HSL 100 Type 2 with Merlin Engines. 120 launches were built and had a top speed of 16 knots. Reports came back from Sea Otters, Avro Ansons and Sunderlands of downed pilots. The rescues were depicted in a film made in 1954 called "The Sea Shall Not Have Them" with Burt Lancaster and Michael Redgrave. The RAF needed to save and keep pilots. There was another film made in the 1944 called "For Those in Peril" with Michael Bacon This shows how the Royal Navy and Air Force worked together with Coastal Command "Walrus" seaplane.

"For Those In Peril"

"The Sea Shall Not Have Them"

HSL 164 with RAF Hurricane

Chain Home Radar System
From Bentley Priory to Stanmore (Group 11 HQ)

Bawdsey Manor

Sir Robert Watson-Watt

The Chain Home Radar System was developed in 1935 by Robert Watson-Watt as an early warning system to detect enemy aircraft, height, numbers and distance, first experiments at Bawdsey Manor.

The early radar was taken up by the Tizard Committee on the 28th of January 1935,

Chain Home radar installation

(secretary Albert Percival Rowe) on behalf of the Air Ministry. Further development occurred in Daventry by Arnold Wilkins and a full system introduced by Patrick Blackett using 5 radar stations.

The early radar range was 30 miles using equipment from Metropolitan Vickers called Con System Type 2. From the Chain Home radar stations signals (21 masts) went to the Filter Room at Bentley Priory alone and then to the HQ control room at Stanmore with reports from the Royal Observer Corps. A second system existed called Chain Home Low which was developed for inland reporting.

Chain Home Radar Stations 1939 AMES Types 1 & 2

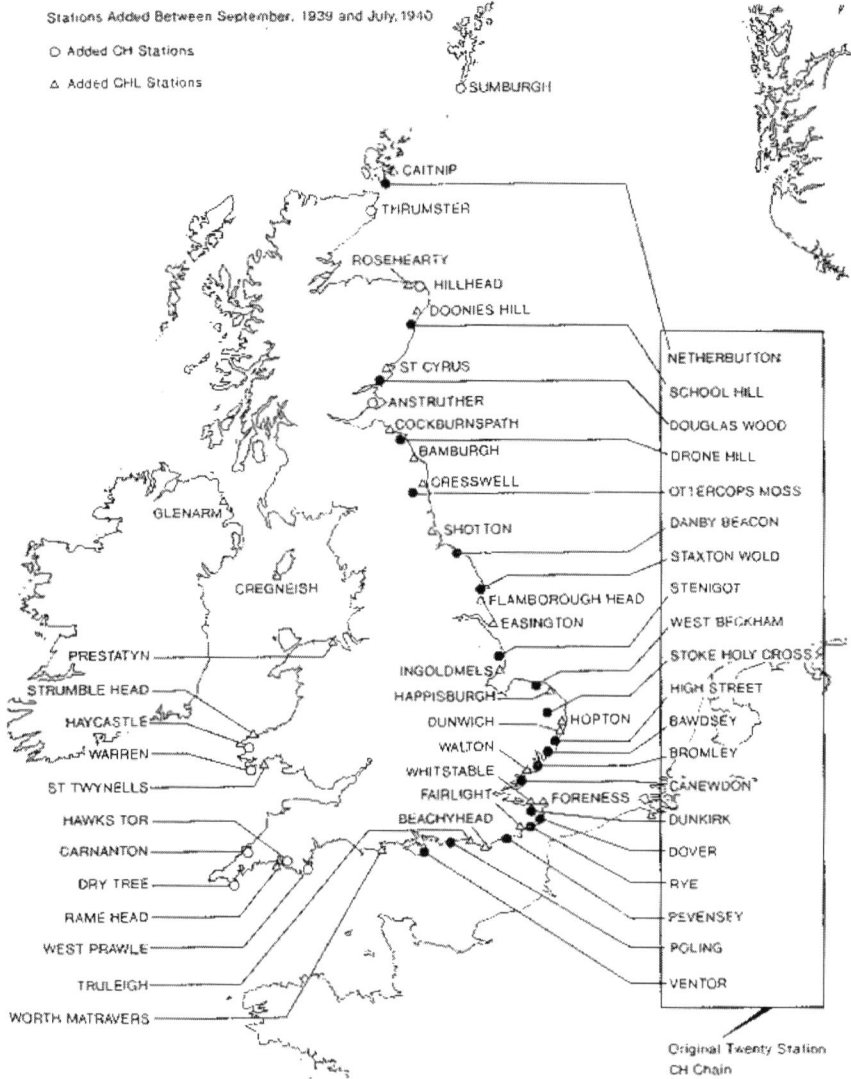

Stations Added Between September, 1939 and July, 1940

O Added CH Stations

△ Added CHL Stations

SUMBURGH

CAITNIP

THRUMSTER

ROSEHEARTY

HILLHEAD

DOONIES HILL

ST CYRUS

ANSTRUTHER

COCKBURNSPATH

BAMBURGH

CRESSWELL

SHOTTON

GLENARM

CREGNEISH

FLAMBOROUGH HEAD

EASINGTON

PRESTATYN

STRUMBLE HEAD

HAYCASTLE

WARREN

ST TWYNELLS

HAWKS TOR

CARNANTON

DRY TREE

RAME HEAD

WEST PRAWLE

TRULEIGH

WORTH MATRAVERS

INGOLDMELS

HAPPISBURGH

DUNWICH

WALTON

WHITSTABLE

FAIRLIGHT

FORENESS

BEACHYHEAD

HOPTON

NETHERBUTTON

SCHOOL HILL

DOUGLAS WOOD

DRONE HILL

OTTERCOPS MOSS

DANBY BEACON

STAXTON WOLD

STENIGOT

WEST BECKHAM

STOKE HOLY CROSS

HIGH STREET

BAWDSEY

BROMLEY

CANEWDON

DUNKIRK

DOVER

RYE

PEVENSEY

POLING

VENTOR

Original Twenty Station CH Chain

Group 11 - South East

Beachy Head, Bembridge, Dunkirk, Dover, Fairlight, Foreness, Poling, Rye, Ventnor, St Lawrence, Woody Bay.

Group 10 - South West and Wales

Worth Matravers, East Cliff Bournemouth, Westcliff Portland, Beer Head Devon, Kingwear Devon, Rame Head Cornwall, Pen Oliver Lizard Cornwall, Trevose Head Cornwall, Dunderhole Point Tintagel, Hartland Point Devon, Swansea Bay, Great Orme Llandudno, Strumble Head Pembrokeshire.

Group 12 - East

Bard Hill Holt Norfolk, Covehithe Suffolk, Dunwich Suffolk, Goldsborough Whitby, Happisburgh Norfolk, Hopton Norfolk, Kessingland Suffolk, Thorpeness Suffolk, Warden Point Isle of Sheppey, Walton Essex.

Group 13 - North

Bamburgh Northumberland, Bempton Yorkshire, Peterhead, Crannoch Hill Banff, Cresswell Northumberland, Dunnet Head, Easington, Goldsborough, Kenley Hill Seaham, Navidale Helmsdale, Ravenscar Yorkshire, St Bees Head Cumberland, Westburn Aberdeen.

All linked to Stanmore Control, Uxbridge. Radar detected aircraft down to 150 metres, some radar stations were built in late 1940 (45 stations) and by 1941 there were 108 AMES Type 2 replacements.

Chain Home Radar System

How the system worked – the radar system was developed from 1940 onwards but was a Low Frequency Radar system that measured the heights of aircraft and the ranges.

The system required a power supply and was later developed into the Dowding system. They were called RDF stations. The transmitting system sent out a signal or radio wave, this hit an object and was bounced back via the tall radio masts, see photo. The signal coming back would have a shorter radio length and could therefore detect and give a pulse of the object on a receiving screen. The equipment in the control room would also detect the height of the object.

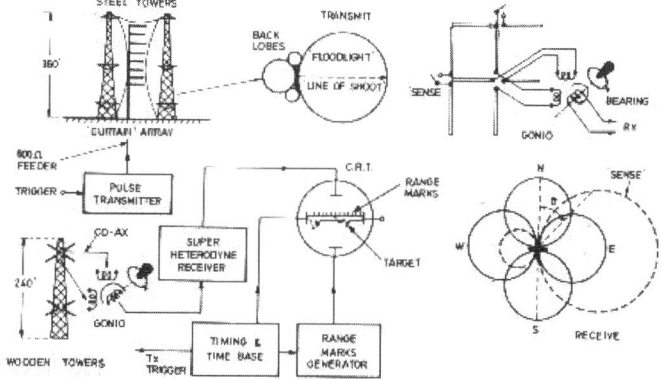

Fig. 1. Principles of CH (Chain Home) R.D.F. system

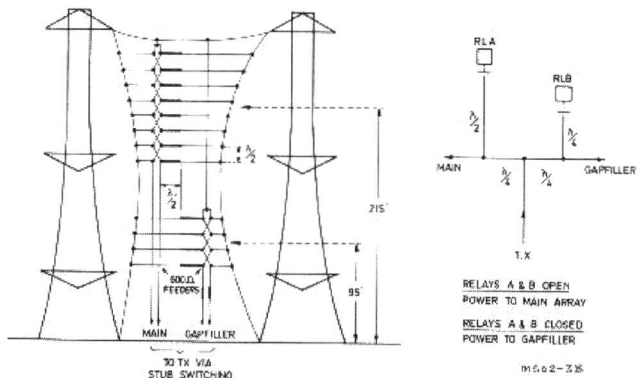

Fig. 3. (a) CH transmitter array (b) stub switching

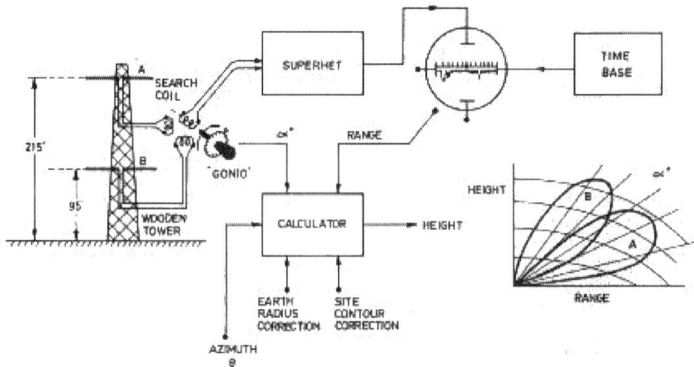

Fig. 4. The principles of CH height-finding

The signals were recorded and then sent up to the central plotting room at RAF sector stations who then transmitted the signals to Stanmore. The Royal Observer Corps were also used to verify

Receiver Room

enemy aircraft movements (see chapter on the Observer Corps). The Dowding System follows in Chapter 3.

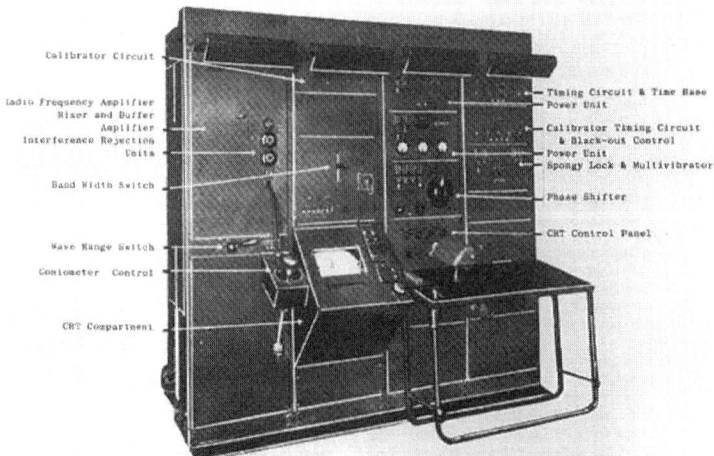

Fig. 13. East Coast receiver RF7

Chapter 3
Dowding System of Air Defence
Organised by Patrick Blackett in 1939

The Dowding Control System developed prior to 1939, (see diagram), consisted of Chain Radar Stations which picked up numbers (source), limited height and direction (this information was sent to the Filter Room at Bentley Priory). The Observer Corps verified direction and height to secure images and the type of aircraft (they had to be good at plane recognition) and information. This information was passed to Fighter HQ at Stanmore. Fighter HQ verified the data from Bentley Priory and the Royal Observer Corps, then passed the information to Group Controller at HQ at Stanmore. This information was put on a plotting table and squadrons allocated to intercept the enemy once the numbers, heights and direction had been established. Squadrons were put on standby and then ordered to scramble, patrol or attack.

Chain Home UK coverage

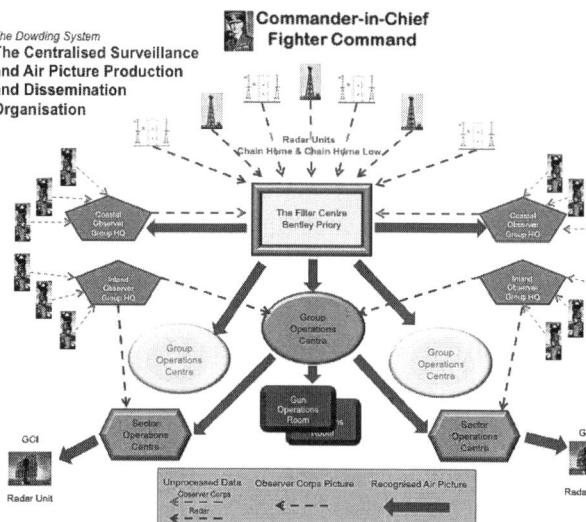

Diagram of Dowding System

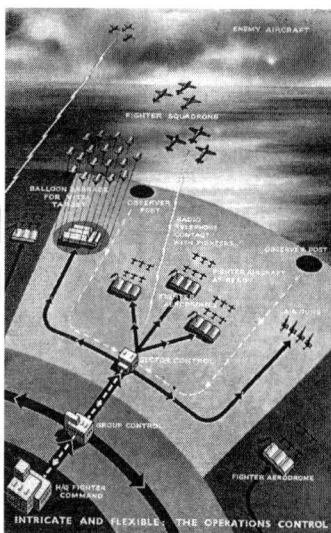

Operations Control

Chain Home radar installation at Poling, Sussex

Chain Home radar masts - Ventor

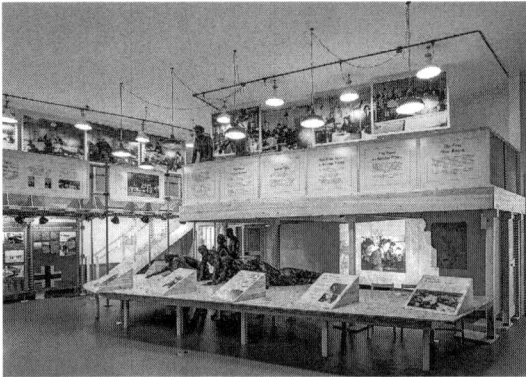

Filter Room at Bentley Priory

Group 11 HQ Stanmore Control

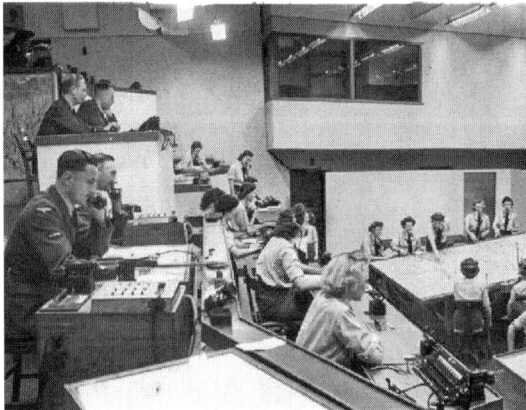

10 Group Fighter Operations Room

Entrance to Stanmore HQ

Royal Observer Corps HQ and Bentley Priory HQ
Air Commodore Alfred Warrington-Morris.

The job of the Royal Observer Corps was to support the
Chain Home radar system, identify by plane recognition,
the type of aircraft, verify height and the compass bearing
that the enemy aircraft were travelling in, and report to the
Sector Command Centre and Fighter Command HQ at
RAF Stanmore. Other duties included air raid siren warn-
ings. All observers were trained at RAF Thorney Island and
were volunteers. The Observer Corps was broken down
into various sectors (see map). The level of command was

*Air Commodore
Warrington-Morris*

similar to the RAF, and personnel were stationed at control centres as plotters and other duties, mainly used to verify direction of travel and height,
using a Pantograph and compass table. All matters were reported to the
Filter Room at Bentley Priory. There were 30,000 observers in 1940.

*Royal Observer Corps
surveillance*

*Royal Observer Corps look
out for enemy aeroplanes*

ROC using the Pantograph

*ROC Fighter Command
surveillance*

Air raid siren

*Royal Observer Corps on duty on
the South Coast.*

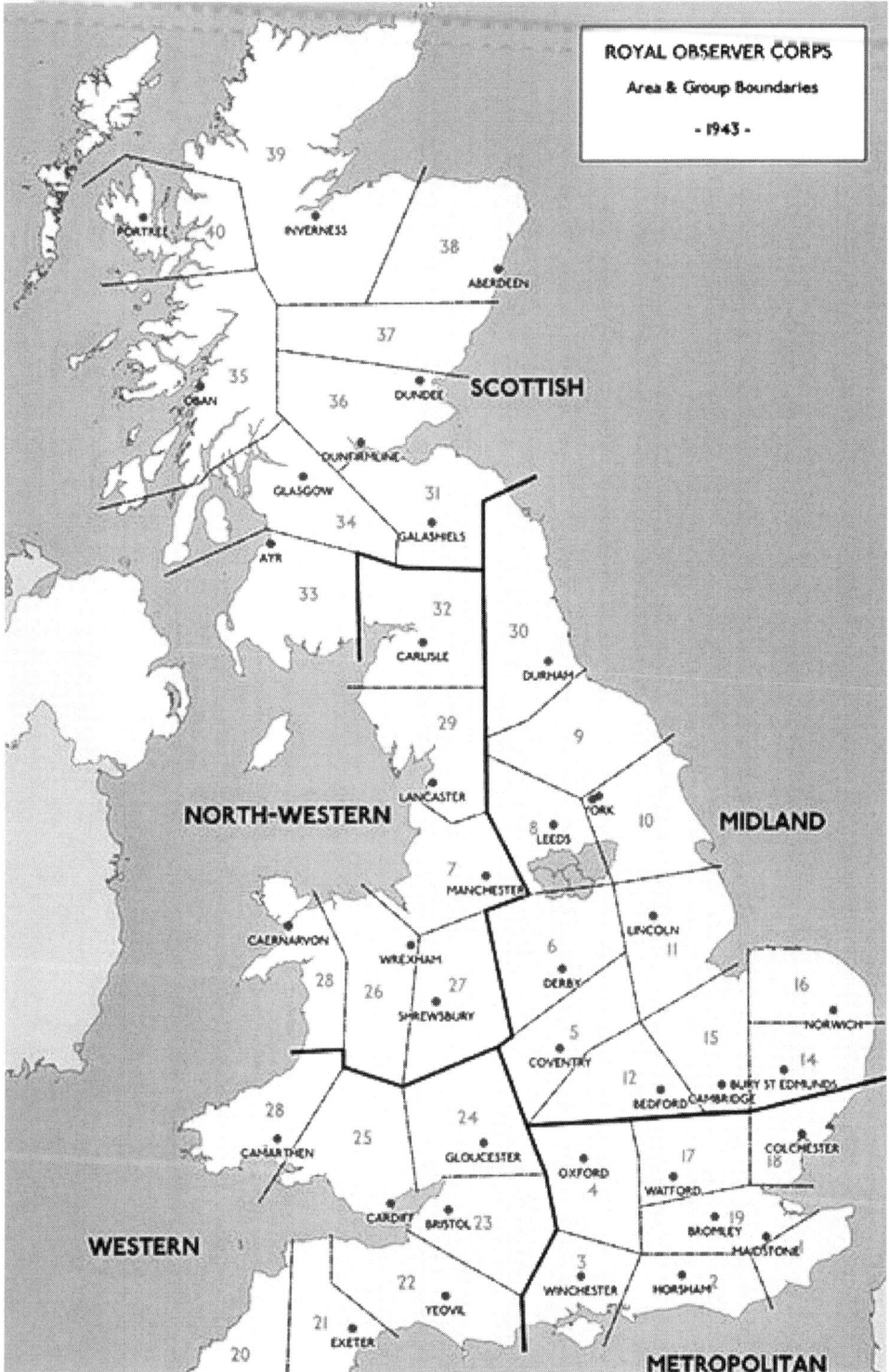

ROC Area and Group Boundaries

RAF Bentley Priory

*Royal Observer
Corps Badge*

Aircraft Recognition data

*Women in the ROC
Fighter Command*

Royal Observer Corps – Area and Group Boundaries

Metropolitan Sector
Group 1 - Maidstone HQ
Group 2 - Horsham
Group 3 - Oxford
Group 4 - Colchester
Group 5 - Bromley
Group 11 - Watford
Midland Sector
Group 6 - Norwich
Group 7 - Bedford
Group 8 - Coventry
Group 15 - Lincoln HQ
Group 18 - Cambridge
Group 19 - Durham
Group 23 - Leeds
Group 26 - Bury St Edmunds

Group 35 - Derby
Group 20- York
Western Sector
Group 9 - Yeovil
Group 10 - Exeter
Group 11 - Truro
Group 12 - Bristol HQ
Group 13 - Carmarthen
Group 14 - Cardiff
Group 15 - Gloucester
North Western Sector
Group 16 - Shrewsbury
Group 17 - Wrexham
Group 18 - Caernarfon
Group 19 - Manchester
Group 20 - Lancaster

Group 21 - Preston Nat. HQ
Group 22 - Carlisle
Group 31 - Belfast
Scottish Sector
Group 24 - Edinburgh HQ
Group 25 - Ayr
Group 27 - Galashiels
Group 28 - Dundee
Group 29 - Aberdeen
Group 30 - Inverness
Group 31 - Glasgow
Group 32 - Dunfermline
Group 33 - Portree
Group 34 - Oban

Chapter 4
Airfield Defence Units
A: Royal Artillery Unit, Anti Aircraft Units, Anti Aircraft Corps.
Sir Frederick Pile – Anti-Aircraft Divisions

1st AA Division - HQ RAF Uxbridge - Major General Robert Crossman

2nd AA Division - HQ RAF Hucknall, Nottinghamshire - East Anglia

3rd AA Division - HQ Edinburgh

4th AA Division - HQ Chester

5th AA Division - HQ Reading

6th AA Division - HQ Existing Division

7th AA Division - HQ Newcastle

8th AA Division - HQ Bristol - South West

9th AA Division - HQ Cardiff - Wales

10th AA Division - HQ covering Yorkshire & Humber

11th AA Division - Covering West and Central Midlands

12th AA Division - Covering South Western Scotland

Anti-Aircarft Division logo

The Groups covering RAF Airfields were:

No 1 AA Division covering RAF 10 and 11 Groups

No 2 AA Division covering RAF 12 Group

No 3 AA Division covering RAF 13 Group

1st AA Division was based at Hillingdon House RAF Uxbridge, under Major General Crossman

A–26th London Anti -Aircraft Brigade - Brigadier Robert Whittaker consisted on 53rd City of London Anti-Aircraft Regiment, 86th HAC Anti-Aircraft Regiment, 88th Anti-Aircraft Regiment.

B–28th Thames & Medway Anti-Aircraft Brigade - 55th (163rd Tunbridge Wells, 166th Rochester, 205th Chatham & Faversham, 307th Tunbridge Wells) and 58th Kent Anti-Aircraft Regiment (Erith, 264th Dartford, 265th Chatham, 268th Maidstone) 61st Anti-Aircraft (170th & 195th Finchley, 171st Pentonville, 272nd Southgate) and 29th Kent Searchlight Regiment (569th Chatham) Lt Col Grover (HQ Chatham, 313rd Chatham, 314th Tonbridge, 322nd Greenhithe, 347th Sidcup) 313th AA -Gillingham, 314th Tonbridge, 317th Hendon, 468th Dover.

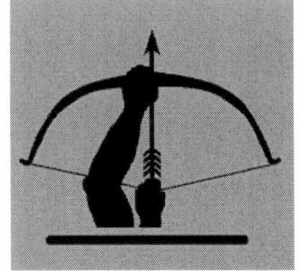

C–38th Light Anti-Aircraft Brigade - Chelsea - 26th Searchlight Regiment, 26th Anti-Aircraft Battalion, 27th AA Battalion, 75th Searchlights HQ Dover (223rd Folkestone, 233rd Dover, 306th Ashford).

D–48th Anti-Aircraft Brigade - 54th, 60th, 97th and 99th Anti-Aircraft Regiments.

E–49th Anti-Aircraft Brigade - 51st, 52nd and 84th Anti-Aircraft Regiments, 89th HQ Sittingbourne (205th Sittingbourne, 234th Deal, 235th Margate).

2nd AA Division was based in Nottinghamshire HQ

A–27th (Home Counties) AA Group HQ RAF Kenley - 60th Anti-Aircraft Regiment, 30th Surrey Searchlights, 31st London Searchlights, 34th Kent Searchlights, 35th Surrey Anti-Aircraft and Searchlights.

B–29th (Anglian) AA Group HQ RAF North Weald - 59th Essex Anti-Aircraft, 28th Essex Searchlights, 33rd St Pancras Searchlights, 36th Anti-Aircraft.

Anti-aircraft guns   *4.5 inch AA gun Kent, 1941*   *Anti-aircraft searchlight*

3rd AA Division

The units had searchlights and anti-aircraft guns, usually Bofors guns, they trained at Thorney Island and each unit had WAAF personnel attached, a breakdown of batteries manning each airfield follows, dependent on the size of airfield, this depends on the anti-aircraft guns on each RAF base.

The 6th Anti Aircraft Division headquarters looked after co-ordination for the 1st and 2nd Divisions coinciding with RAF Sectors Debden, North Weald, Hornchurch, Biggin Hill and Kenley for Fighter Group 11. Coastal batteries extended from Lowestoft to Worthing. AA defences consisted of (1) HAA units Medway North (North of Thames Estuary) and Medway South (South of Thames, defending Chatham and Rochester), this included defence of airfields.(2) LAA guns additional protection vulnerable areas, Air Ministry Experimental Stations, Fighter Aerodromes, Dockyards, Oil Depots, Magazines, Industrial areas and factories.

(1)–HAA Units (Heavy Guns)

Three types of Guns - 3 inch, 3.7 inch and 4.5 inch as follows:
(Total number of men per battery = 105)

BATTERY	GUNS
Harwich	3in x8; 3.7in x15
Thames North	3in x12; 3.7in x8; 4.5in x32
Thames South	3in x14; 3.7in x32; 4.5in x32
Dover and Manston	3in x16; 3.7in x12
Biggin Hill	3in x4
North Weald	3in x6; 3.7in x4
Wattisham	3in x4

Bofors gun crew ready for action

(2) Airfields LAA (Light Anti Aircraft Units)

Searchlight, Balloons SQ

AIRFIELDS	No. AUG	BRIGADES	No. SEP
Debden	4	41st AA Brigade, 30th Surrey Searchlight Bal 904	21
Wattisham	12	35th AA Brigade, 30th Surrey Searchlight Bal 904	12
Biggin Hill	5	88th AA Brigade, 30th Surrey Searchlight Bal 904	9
Manston	8	58th AA Brigade, 29th Searchlights, Balloons ?	8
West Malling	12	58th AA Brigade, 29th Searchlights, Balloons 961	14
Croydon	12	148th AA Brigade, 30th Searchlights, Balloons ?	12
Kenley	12	27th AA Brigade , 30th Searchlights, Balloons ?	14
Redhill	0	Machine Gun Posts, Searchlights ?, Ball Store No 24	3
Gravesend	8	265th AA Brigade, 26th Searchlights, Balloons 952	4
Shorts (Rochester)	0	166th AA Brigade, Searchlights ?, Balloons 952nd	15
Detling	2	67th (268, 265 Batt), 26th Searchlights, Balloon 961	16
Eastchurch	0	Machine Gun Posts, 46th East Surrey Balloon 961	12
Hawkinge	8	26th AA Brigade, 233rd Searchlights, Balloons 952	8
Lympne	0	Machine Gun Posts, 223rd Searchlights, Ball 952nd	2
North Weald	15	59th Essex AA, 28th Searchlights, Balloons 910th	13
Martlesham	14	59th Essex AA, 28th Essex Searchlights, Balloons?	15
Rochford	10	59th Essex AA, 28th Essex Searchlights, Ball 910th	16
Hornchurch	10	33rd AA Brigade, 28th Glasgow Highlanders, 910th	12
Stapleford Abbots	0	Machine Gun Posts, Searchlights ?, Balloons ?	2

RADAR STATIONS	No. AUG	BRIGADES	No. SEP
Darsham	9		10
Dunkirk	9		10
Rye	9		14
Pevensey	9		24
Bawdsey	0		6
Gt Bromley	0		14
Canewdon	7		15
RNAS STATIONS			
Gosport		Machine Gun Posts 8th Hampshire C Company	
Lee on Solent		8th AA Division, unknown units ?, Searchlights etc.	
Pembroke		9th AA Division, Bofors Gun Tower, Sqn No21 Balloons	
Portland		Bofors Gun Tower, plus HMS Foylebank	

Barrage Balloon Units Anti Aircraft Units
HQ Old Church Lane, Stanmore and RAF Cardington
Commander Air Vice Marshal Owen Tudor Boyd

The purpose of barrage balloons was to stop and disrupt air attacks on ground targets. Training occurred on barrage balloons at RAF Cardington, there were (?) people in each flight for each squadron, 5 flights of 9 barrage balloons each, so each squadron had 45 barrage balloons. The barrage balloons were filled with pumped oxygen from a compressor and launched from a purpose-built truck. The squadron numbers (next page) and also the balloon centres where they were stored.

RAF Balloon Command badge

RAF Cardington Balloon Shed

WAAF balloon operators report for inspection before going off duty

Squadron Numbers

901 Kidbroke, 902 Brixton, 903 Forest Hill, 952 Sheerness, 961 Dover, also 904-999 different locations (Too many to list here). Usually 45 balloons per squadron attached to airfields (15 per flight, 3 flights).

Balloon Centres (for storing balloons)

No 30: 1 Kidbroke, 2 Chessington, 3 Stanmore, 4 Chigwell, 22 Biggin Hill, 23 Gravesend, 23 Redhill.

No 31: 5 Sutton Coldfield, 6 Wythall, 7 Alvaston, 8 Fazakerly (Liverpool), 9 Warrington, 10 Middleton(Manchester).

No 32: 11 Pucklechurch (Bristol), 12 Tichfield, 13 Yealhampton, 14 Ely (Cardiff), 21 Pembroke Dock.

No 33: 15 Forest Hill (Newcastle), 16 Norton (Sheffield), 17 Sutton on Hull.

No 34: 18 Bishop Briggs (Glasgow), 19 Rosyth.

Barrage Balloons over London

The Fordson Barrage Balloon Winch

RAF Balloon Command in operation

WAAF for duty with the RAF

Barrage balloon being inflated

RAF Regiments and RAF Provost Units

These units protected the airfields security, manned the guard rooms and patrolled the perimeter fences. Each RAF airfield had its own detachments of personnel to man the guardhouse and perimeter. The RAF Regiment and Provost units were not formed until 1942 and trained at Alma Park (previously known as Belton Park, Grantham).

Airfield Control Operations Rooms

Depending on the size of the airfield and the number of personnel, the operations room and control room, some of the observer corps were on the surface looking out for Enemy Aircraft. Usually there were 31 personnel in a sector control room, a number of WAAF plotters and telephone operators – dependent on Sector Station.

Group 11 HQ Stanmore Control

Lascaris Map

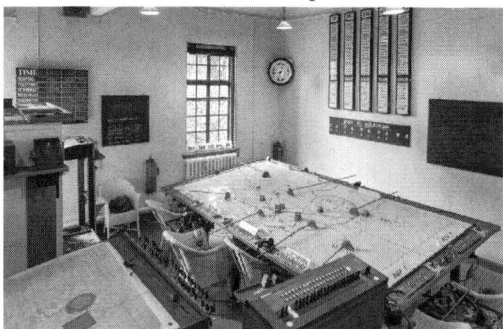

1940 Operations Room

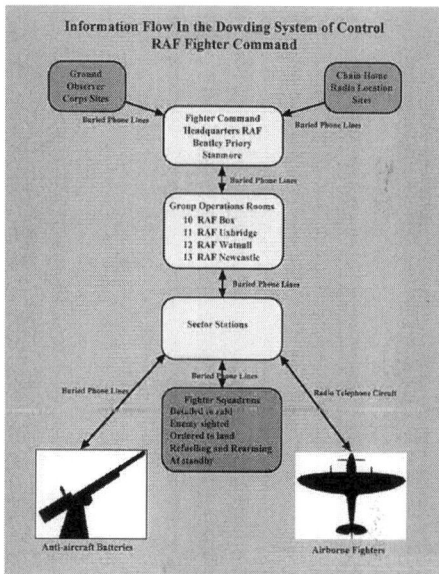

Information Flow In the Dowding System of Control RAF Fighter Command

Dowding system

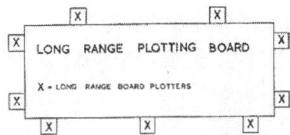

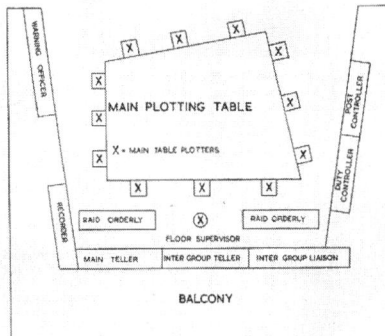

Plotting layout

Chapter 5

Airfield Support Units
Maintenance of Aircraft & Airfields

A. Air Maintenance and Ground Crew to repair aircraft.

Engineers were either attached to the squadron, armourers or aircraft fitters and riggers. Aircraft were flown to special units around the country –

No.1 MU Repairs (Maintenance Unit) Kidbrooke and Netheravon,

No.2 Ammunition Broadheath, Bridleway or Sealand,

No.3 Aircraft Equipment -RAF Milton,

No.4 Repairs RAF West Ruislip,

No.5 Aircraft Storage RAF Kemble,

No.6 MU repairs Blenheims, Fairey Battles, Spitfires, Oxfords - RAF Brize Norton,

No.7 Equipment RAF Quedgeley.

The RAF repair crews could fix aircraft quickly and repaired runways quickly within 24 hours.

RAF Fighter Command - Armourers

RAF Fighter Command - Fitters & Riggers

Peter Townsend with Ground Crew

B. Airfield Operations and Control.

Mess Rooms (Cooks, Waiters), Administration (Telephones, Messengers, Drivers, Cleaners, Hairdressers, Quartermasters, Paymasters, Personnel, Records).

These duties were carried out by trained personnel, some special squadrons were set up for training, WAAFs performed a lot of these duties to allow men to fulfil front line roles.

C. Number of Personnel on Average RAF Airfield

(Air Crew average not included. Station number based on RAF Detling Operational Records.)

HQ STAFF	OFFICERS	AIRMEN	WAAFs	CIVILIANS	TOTAL
Commandant/Wng-Cdr	1	1			2
Operations Room	13	6		12	31
Signal Section	1	27		3	31
Equipment Section	1	9		3	13
Accounting Section	1	5		2	8
Workshops	1	8		2	11
WAAF various	5		59		64
Other HQ Staff	4	95		10	109
Sub Total	**27**	**151**	**59**	**32**	**269**
ANTI AIRCRAFT UNITS					
268-67 Battery	4	106			110
265.67 Battery	5	117			122
ROYAL ENGINEERS					
RE 703	1	67			68
RE 513	1	6			7
AA 53	2	40			42
Balloons Units	5	216			221
Sub Total	**9**	**329**			**338**
TOTAL	**36**	**480**		**32**	**607**

Engine maintenance

Rearming a Spitfire

Rearming and refueling a Hurricane

Women's Auxiliary Air Force (WAAF)
HQ West Drayton, Uxbridge.
Commandant Air Commodore Jane Trefusis Forbes

Jane Trefusis Forbes DBE

WAAF was set up on the 21st of June 1939, 48 companies of 150 women per company. Training occurred at 5 main sites and 2 additional sites. The women were posted to various RAF units and covered the following areas: WAAFs were recruited from existing ATS units.

A1 Personnel, A2 Intelligence, A3 Operations, A4 Logistics and Stores, A5 Strategy & Defence (Balloons & Observers), A6 Communications & Telephones, A7 Training & Organisation, A8 Finance & Budgets, A9 Politics & Legal.

Training Schools

1-West Drayton - Air Operations and Control Room.
2-Harrogate No7 Training School - clerical work.
3-Innsworth, Gloucestershire - Technical Training, Armoury.
4-Wilmslow and RAF Wickenby - Stores & Maintenance, also RAF Handforth, RAF Procedures.
5- Bridgnorth - No 4 Recruit Centre Basic Training and Radio, Wireless and Telephones.
Aircraft Ferrying (Air Transport Auxiliary ATA) was conducted from RAF White Waltham.

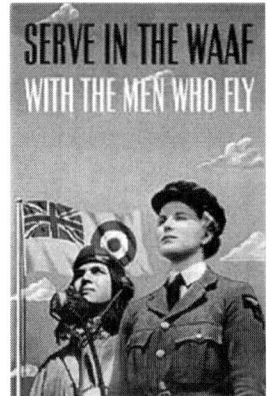

Air Ferry Centres: 1-(HQ) White Waltham; 2-Whitchurch; 3-Harwenden; 4-Prestwick; 5-Thame; 6-Ratcliffe; 7 Sherburn in Elmet; 8-Belfast; 9-Aston Down; 10-Lossiemouth; 12-Cosford; 14-Ringway 15-Hamble; 16-Kirkbride.

Assignments - Postings

WAAF's were posted to the following groups, after initial training:
Group 1 - RAF Bombers,
Group 2 - Blenheims and Combat Support,
Group 11 - Fighter Command and Defence,
Group 22 - Personnel -Training High Wycombe,
Group 38 - (not used until 1944).

RAF Wilmslow

Control Room

Passing out parade

WAAF Recruits

Assisting in bomb inspection

WAAF Aircraft Ferrying

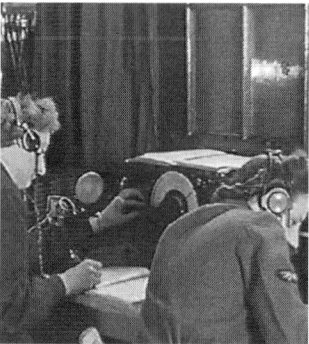

German translators

Radio operator

WAAF operating searchlights

Early warning radar station

Searchlight operators

WAAF radar operators

Chapter 6

German Luftwaffe Organisation France 1940

Commander Field Marshal Oberkommando Hermann Göring – HQ Berlin

Luftwaffe Eagle

Luftwaffe Iron Cross

Commander Field Marshal Herman Göring

The attack on Britain by the Luftwaffe was from 3 German Air Forces:

Luftflotte 2 HQ originally based in Braunschweig, HQ moved to Brussels under Field Marshal Albert Kesselring. This lead the main assault.

Luftflotte 3 HQ originally based in Munich, HQ moved to Paris under Field Marshal Hugo Sperrle. Main thrust was in the West Country.

Luftflotte 5 HQ originally based in Hamburg moved to Stavanger, Norway under Field Marshal Hans-Jurgen Stümpff from 13th of August (Adlertag - Eagle Day).

Albert Kesselring

Hans-Jurgen Stumpff

Hugo Sperrle

Special Unit – Nachtjagdgeschwader 2. Night Fighter Raiders -intruders from 1st September 1940, used to disrupt night flying training and harass bombers over their own airfields. Junkers JU 88 - Obersleutnant Karl Hulshoff, based in Gilze-Rijen in Holland, claimed 143 victories between October 1940 and 1942.

Long range reconnaissance aircraft, Focke-Wulf 200 (The Condor), were used which were also used in the attacks on British-Allied shipping in the first phase of the attacks.

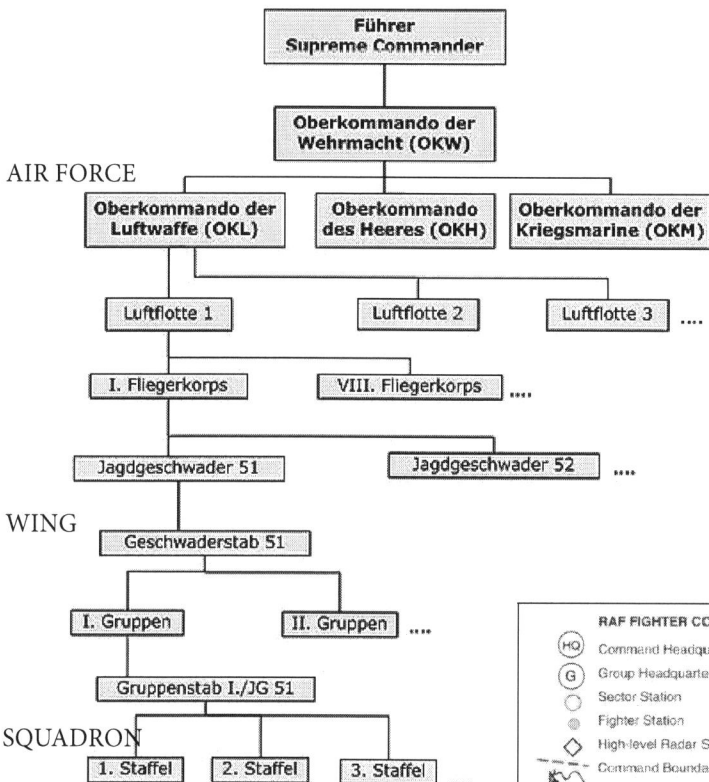

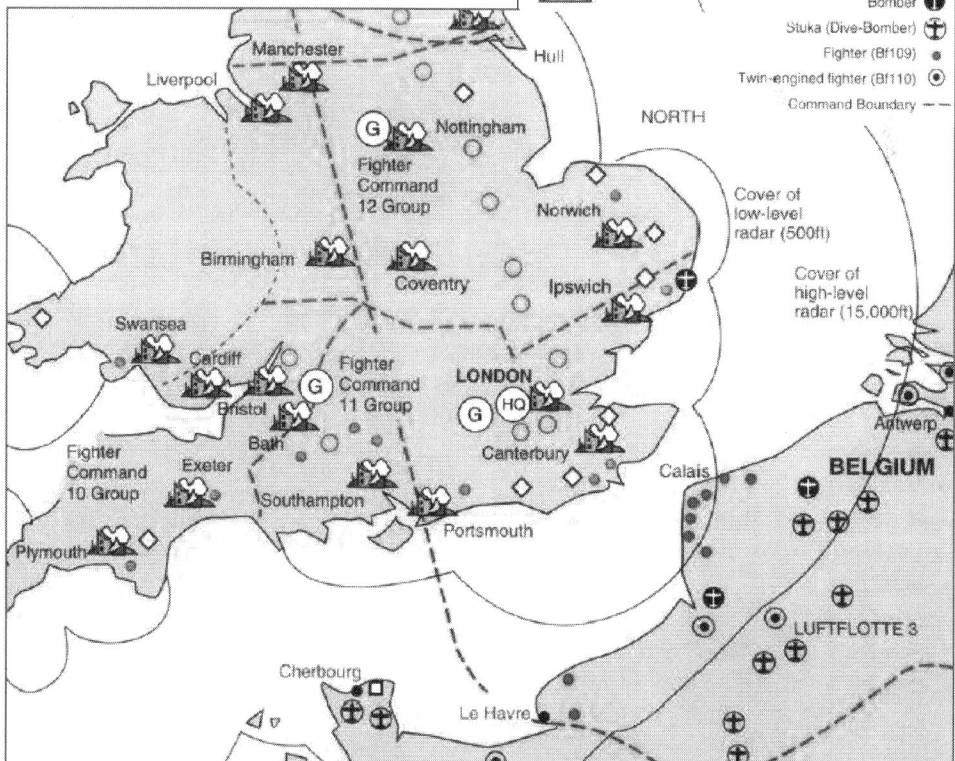

Luftwaffe Air Units for the Battle of Britain
Luftflotte 2: Main Aircraft Dornier, Heinkel and Messerschmitt

1 Fliegerkorps - General Ulrich Grauert - HQ Beauvais

·*Kg1* Kampfgeschwader 1 - Rosières-en-Santerre - Gr 1 & Gr 2 -Heinkel 111 (Montdider), Gr 3 Junker JU88 111 (Rosières). Kg1 Commander Obersleutnant exSS.

·*Kg76* Kampfgeschwader 76 - Cormeilles-en-Vexin Gr Stab & Gr 3 Dorniers (Cormeilles) Gr 2 Creil Dorniers Gr 1 (Beauvais) Junkers JU88. Commander Obersleut. Stefan Frölich

·*Auf122* Aufklärungstruppe 122 - (Reconnaissance) Junkers, Dorniers, Heinkel - (Haute-Fontaine)

2 Fliegerkorps General Bruno Loerzer HQ Ghent

·*Kg2* Kampfgeschwader 2 - Arras Gr 1 Dornier (Epinoy), Gr 2 Dorniers (Arras), Gr 3 Dornier (Cambrai) - Commander Oberst Johannes Fink.

·*Kg3* Kampfgeschwader 3 - Le Culot Gr 1 Dornier (Le Culot), Gr 2 Dornier (Deurne), Gr 3 Dornier (Sint-Truiden) - Commander Oberst Wolfgang von Chamier-Glisczinski.

·*Kg53* Kampfgeschwader 53 - Lille Gr 1 Heinkel, Gr 2 Heinkel, Gr 3 Heinkel all in Airfield (Lille North) - Commander Oberst Wolf-JÜrgen Stahl.

·*Sig1* Sturzkamfgeschwader 1 - Pas de Calais Staffel 1, 2, 3 Messerschmitt 110 and 109 (Calais - Marck) - Commander Hauptmann Anton Keil.

·Leh2 Lehrgeschwader 2 - Calais Gr 1, Gr 2 Messerschmitt 109 (Leeuwarden, Calais), Gr 7-9 Messerschmitt 110 (Ghent, Brussels)

5 Fliegerkorps General Joachim Coeler - HQ Soesterberg, Belgium

·*Kg4* Kampfgeschwader 4 - Soesterberg Gr 1 Heinkel (Soesterberg), Gr2 Heinkel (Eindhoven) Gr 3 Junkers (Amsterdam) - Commander Oberst Hans-Joachim Rath.

·*Kg100* Kampfgruppe 100 - Pathfinder Bombers Heinkel He111 (Vannes)

·*Ku126* Kustenfliergruppe 126 - Minelaying Heinkel 111 (Various)

·*Auf122* Aufklärungsgruppe 122 Eindhoven Junkers

2 Jagfliegerfürher 2 - Generalmajor Theodore Wissant - HQ Samer

·*Jag3* Jagdgeschwader 3 - Samer Gr 1 Messerschmitt 109 (Colembert), Gr 2 Messerschmitt 109 (Samer) Gr 3 Messerschmitt 109 (Desvres) - Commander Oberst Karl Viek.

·*Jag26* Jagdgeschwader 26 - Audembert all Messerschmitt 109 Gr1 (Audembert) Gr2 (Marquise) Gr3 (Caffiers) Commanders Maj Gotthard Handrick & Adolf Galland.

·*Jag51* Jagdgeschwader 51 - Wissant all Messerschmitt 109 Gr1 (Wissant), Gr2 (Wissant) Gr 3 (St Omer) Commanders - Oberst Theo Osterkamp then Maj Werner Mölders.

·*Jag52* Jagdgeschwader 52 - Coquelles all Messerschmitt 109 Gr 1 (Coquelles) Gr 2 (Peuplingues) - Commander Hanns TrÜbenbach

·*Jag54* Jagdgeschwader 54 - Campagne all Messerschmitt 109 Gr 1 (Guînes) Gr 2 (Hermelinghen) Gr 3 (Guînes) - Commander Major Martin Mettig

·*Leh2* Lehrgeschwader 2 - Calais Marck Messerschmitt 109 Gr 1 (Calais -Marck) - Commander Hauptmann Herbert Ihlefeld.

·*Zer26* Zerstörergeschwader 26 - Lille all Messerschmitt 110 Stab (Lille), Gr1 (Yvrench) Gr 2 (Crecy) Gr 3 (Barley) Comdr Oberst Joachim-Friedrich Huth Gr1 & 2 moved to St Omer.

·*Zer76* Zerstörergeschwader 76 - Laval all Messerschmitt 110 Stab (Laval) Gr 2 (Abbeville Gr 3 (Laval) - Commander Oberst Walter Grabmann.

Luftflotte 3: Versailles HQ France from August 13th Hugo Sperrle

4 Fliegerkorps - General Kurt Pflugbeil HQ Dinard

·**Leh1** Lehrgeschwader 1 - Orleans all Junkers JU88 Gr 1 and Gr 2 (Orleans Bricy) Gr 3 (Chateaudun)
·**Kg27** Kampfgeschwader 27 - Tours all Heinkel HE111 Gr 1 (Tours) Gr 2 Dinard) Gr 3 (Rennes)
·**Kg40** Kampfgeschwader 40 Brest Stab Junkers 88 (Brest-Guipavas), Gr 1 Focke-Wulfe 200 (Brest - Guipavas)
·**Sig3** Sturzkampfgeschwader 3 Caen - Stabachwarne Junkers 88 (Caen)
·**Kg806** Kampfgeschwader 806 Nantes - Junkers 88 (Nantes),
·**Auf31** Aufklarungsgruppe 31 Reconnaissance - Dornier, Junkers, Messerschmitt (Rennes)
·**Auf131** Aufklarungsgruppe 131 as above Junkers JU88 (North West France)

7 Fliegerkorps - Gen Robert Ritter von Greim HQ Orly Paris

·**Kg51** Kampfgeschwader 51 Orly all Junkers JU88 Gr1 (Melun) Gr 2 (Orly) Gr 3 (Etampes)
·**Kg54** Kampfgeschwader 54 Evreux all Junkers JU88 Gr 1 (Evreux) Gr2 (St Andre de L'Eure)
·**Kg55** Kampfgeschwader 55 Villacoublay all Heinkel HE111 Gr 1 (Dreux) Gr 2 (Chartres) Gr 3 (Villacoublay)
·**Auf14** Aufklärungsgruppe 14 Reconnaissance Dornier & Messerschmidt 110 (Cherbourg)
·**Auf121** Aufklärungsgruppe 121 Reconnaissance Dornier and Junkers (Villacoublay)

8 Fliegerkorps - Gen Freiherr von Richthofen HQ Deauville

·**Sig1** Sturzkampfgeschwader 1 Angers all Junkers JU87 Gr 1 and Gr 2 (Angers)
·**Sig2** Sturzkampfgeschwader 2 St Malo all Junkers JU87 Gr 1 (St Malo) Gr 2 (Lannion)
·**Sig77** Sturzkampfgeschwader 77 Caen all Junkers JU87 Gr 1, 2 and 3 (Caen)
·**Leh1** Lehrgeschwader 1 Caen Messerschmitt BF110 (Caen)
·**Auf11** Aufklärungsgruppe 11 Reconnaissance Dornier & Messerschmitt (Bernay)
·**Auf123** Aufklärungsgruppe 123 as above Dorniers & Junkers (Paris)

3 Jagdfliegerführer Oberst Werner Junck HQ Deauville

·**Jag2** Jagdgeschwader 2 Evreux all Messerschmitt 109 Stab Gr 1 Gr (Beaumont le Roger) Gr 3 (Le Havre)
·**Jag27** Jagdgeschwader 27 Cherbourg as above Stab (Cherbourg), Gr 1 (Plumetot),Gr 2 (Crepon) Gr 3 (Carquebut)
·**Jag53** Jagdgeschwader 53 Cherbourg as above Stab (Cherbourg) Gr 1 (rennes) Gr 2(Dinan) Gr 3 Sempy)
·**Zer2** Zerstorergeschwader 2 Toussus le Noble all Messerschmitt 110 Gr 1 (Toussus) Gr 2 (Amiens) Gr 3 (Guyancourt)

Luftflotte 2 Commanders

Jag2 - Oberst Werner Junck; Jag27 - Major Max Ibel; Jag53 - Maj Hans-Jürgen von Cramon-Taubadel;
Zer2 - Oberstleutnant Friedrich Vollbrecht.
Sig1 - Major Walter Hagen; Sig2 - Major Oskar Dinort; Sig77 - Major Clemens Graf von Schönborn
Leh1 & Auf11 - Oberst Alfred Bülowius.
Kg27 - Oberst Hans Behrendt; Kg51 - Oberst Dr Johann-Volkmar Fisser; Kg54 - Oberst Otto Höhne;
Kg55 - Oberst Alois Stoeckl.
Kg100 - (Night attack pathfinder unit) Vannes Hauptmann Friedrich Aschenbrenner.

Luttflotte 5 - Field Marshall Stumffe HQ Stavanger

10- Fliegerkorps General Leut Hans Geisler HQ Stavanger Norway

·Wet10 Wettererkundungskette 10 - Stavanger Heinkel HE 111

·Kg26 Kampfgeschwader 26 - Stavanger all Heinkel 111 Stab, Gr 1 Gr 3 (Stavanger)

·Kg30 Kampfgeschwader 30 - Aalborg all Junkers JU88 Gr 1, 2, 3 and Stab based in (Aalborg)

·Zer76 Zerstörergeschwader 76 -Stavanger Messerschmitt BF110 Gr 1

·Jag77 Jagdgeschwader 77 -Stavanger Gr 2 (Stavanger - Trondheim)

·Ku506 Kustenfliergruppe 506 Stavanger all Heinkel 115 Gr 1 (Stavanger) Gr 2 (Trondheim-Tromsa) Gr 3 (List)

·Auf22 Aufklärungsgruppe 22 Stavanger Dornier DO17

·Auf120 Aufklärungsgruppe 120 Stavanger Reconnaissance Heinkel, Junkers

·Auf Aufklärungsgruppe (as above) Dornier and Messerschmitt 110

·See Seenotdienst - Air-sea Rescue Heinkel HE59 (Sola, Bergen, Trondheim)

Messerschmitt Me 109

Messerschmitt Me 110

Dornier DO 17

Junkers 87 Stuka

Heinkel HE 111

Heinkel HE 177

Luftwaffe Airfield Bases in France & Belgium

LUFTFLOTTE 2 AIRFIELDS	LUFTFLOTTE 3 AIRFIELDS
Amiens	Amiens
Amsterdam (Skipol)	Antwerp
Audembert	Angers
Arques	Beaumont le Roger
Barley	Bernay
Beauvais (Tille airport)	Bourges
Brussels	Brest - Guipavas
Caffiers	Bricy
Calais (Marck)	Caen - Carentan
Calais (Leeuwarden)	Caen - Colleville
Campagne	Carquebut
Cambrai (Niergnies)	Channel Islands: Jersey & Guernsey - Calais
Chamont	Chateaudun
Crecy-en-Ponthieu	Cherbourg - Maupertus
Coquelles	Chartres
Colenbert	Crepon
Courvrose	Deauville
Cormeilles	Dinan
Creil	Dinard
Denain	Dreux
Deurne	Evreux
Desvres	Etampes
Etaples	Florennes
Eindhoven	Guyancourt
Guines	Laval
Gulnes	Lannion
Hermalingen	Le Havre
Laval	Le Mans
Le Culot	Marquise-Ost
Le Havre	Melun
Lille	Nantes
Montreuil	Orleans (Bricy)
Montdidier	Paris (Orly)
Rosieres	Plumetot
Ostermoor	Rennes (Saint Jacques)
St Omer	Sempy
St Pol	St Andre de L'Eure
St Truiden	St Leger
Vannes	St Malo
Wissant	St Trond
	Tours
	Toussus le Noble
	Twenet
	Villacoublay
	Vannes
	Vitrey

German victories were reported in the magazine *SIGNAL* (German Armed Forces) & *Der Adler* (Luftwaffe magazine).

Operation Seelöwe (Sea Lion)
The Invasion of Great Britain
To commence August 10, 1940 – Führer Directive No. 16

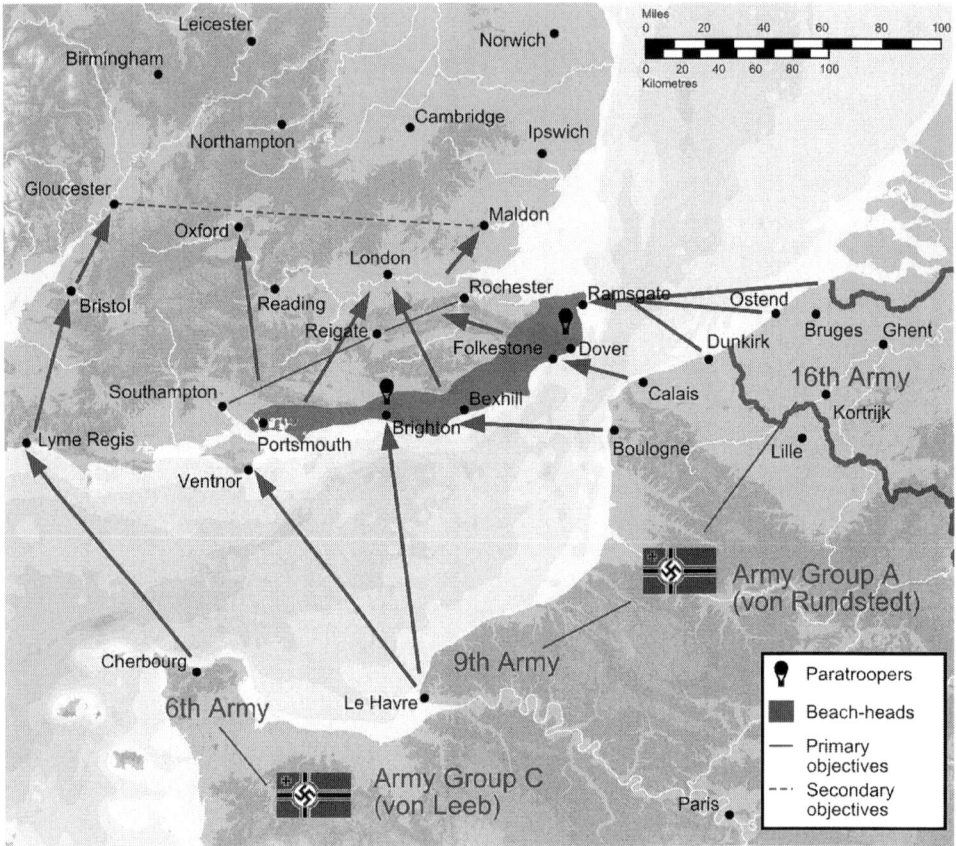

Führer Directive 16 was officially issued for an attack and invasion of the United Kingdom to be launched on the 10th of August 1940. The German Chancellor gave Britain a final ultimatum in July 1940 following the defeat and fall of France in June 1940 and the evacuation from Dunkirk. The above map shows the plans the Germans had to invade. Directive 17 was also issued for instruction to the Luftwaffe to destroy the RAF prior to the invasion. Prior to invasion Paratroopers would land to secure bridgeheads.

The first wave of German troops to land were Army Group A -90,000 men, 650 tanks, 4,500 horses. They were to embark from 1 - Northern Army Group A (Von Rundstedt), 16th German Army - Ostend, Dunkirk, Calais and Cherbourg (required 550 barges, 185 tugs and 370 gunboats) and Army Group C - 170,000 men, 57,500 horses, 34,200 vehicles, 2 - Southern Army Group C (Von Leeb) - Le Havre and Cherbourg (required 760 transport barges, 187 tugs, 574 motorboats, 100 transports), to be sent over 3-4 days. All convoys to be protected by warships against attacks from the Royal Navy. However Directive 17 was also issued to destroy not only the RAF, RNAS but also the Royal Navy dockyards to stop the Royal Navy from sailing.

Army Group A Divisions:

1st Division - Major General Philipp Kleffel - land Romney Marshes.

7th Division - Major General Eccard von Gablenz - land Romney Marshes.

17th Division - Lt General Herbert Loch - land Pevensey Bay, Hastings, and Folkestone.

35th Division - General Hans Wolfgang Reinhard - land Rye.

Reserves

45th Division- General Friedrich Materna.

164th Division - Lt General Joseph Foltmann.

Operation Sea Lion - Adler Paratroops

Preparation for Operation Sea Lion

Invasion barges at Wilhelmshaven.

Operation Sea Lion preparation

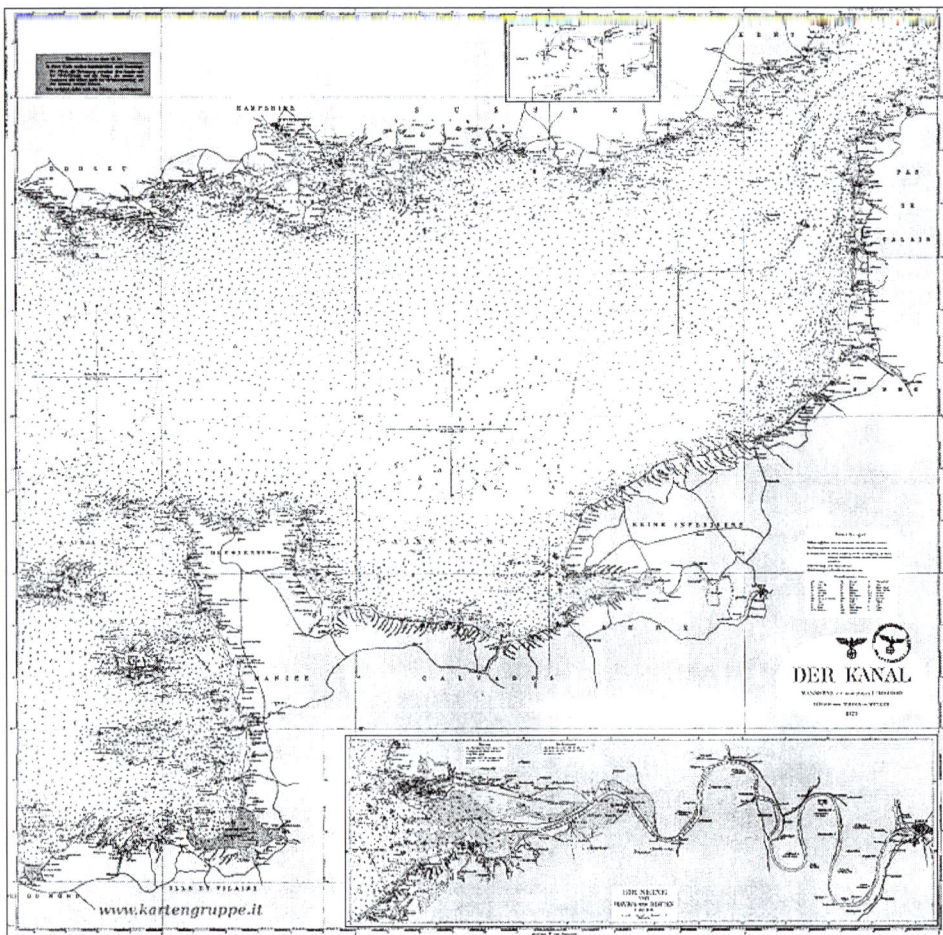

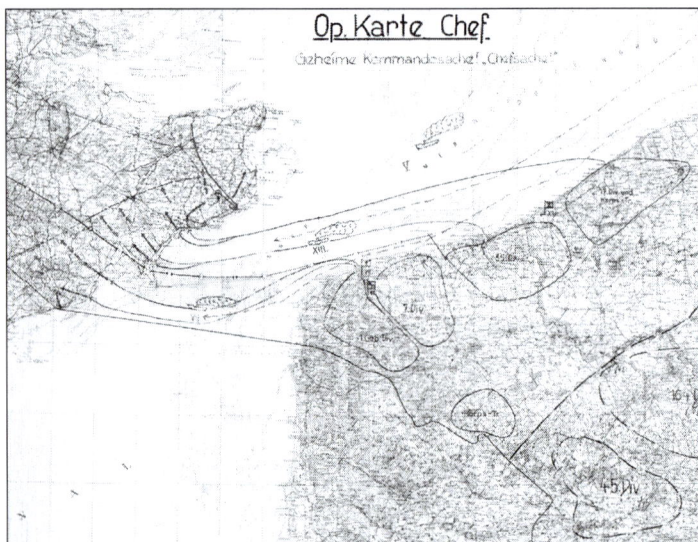

Maps used by the Germans to plan the invasion.

Siebel Ferries to flank the invasion convoys

Landing boat with traction vehicle

*Big Bertha firing on Dover – Hellfire Corner
Long-range gun mounted on a train*

Hitler with Generals

Luftwaffe Target Finding with Knickebein Radar

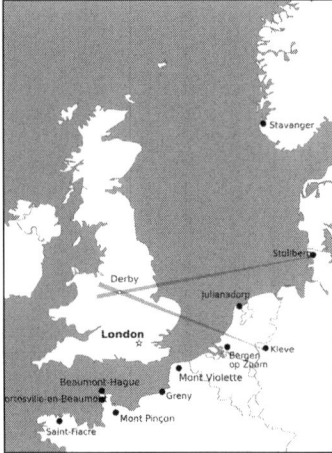

Map of Knickebein transmitters

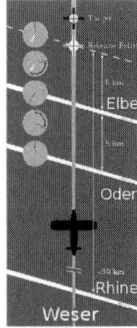

X-Gerät

Lorenz beam

Heinkel over Wapping

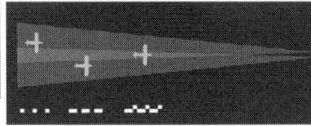

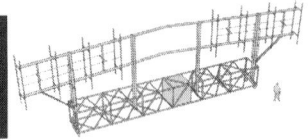

Knickebein Antenna

Knickebein or 'Bent Leg' was developed in 1933 by Doctor Rudolf Kühnold and was a system for finding a target to bomb. Two beams were sent out from transmitting stations and where they crossed was were the bomber should drop its bombs. The signal was picked up in the aircraft. The Royal Aircraft Establishment at Farnborough picked up that the Germans had this system in 1939 (Dr Jones) and code named it 'Headache'. Counter measures were developed code named 'Aspirin' and fitted equipment to Avro Ansons. However at the start of the Battle of Britain none of the equipment had been deployed. The Germans were using this equipment in the Battle of Britain. Once our counter measures were working, the systems took Knickebein and developed two further system a) X-Gerät and then b) Y-Gerät.

German Secret Service Abwehr involvement
Admiral Canaris - Kriegsmarine HQ Hamburg

To find out information on RAF and RNAS airfields and targets, the German secret service had over 130 agents operating in England (under the Twenty Committee, MI5 and Bletchley Park broke the Enigma Code and found and tracked the agents), Nazi sympathisers (Oswald Mosley followers). They sent in a further 25 agents in June to perform Operation Lena to gather intelligence on British Coastal Defences and Airfields, in particular Sam McCarthy (code name 'Biscuit') and Arthur Owens a Welsh Nationalist (code named Snow). MI5 found the names of the agents (Sir Vernon Kell) and followed up 8,200 vetting requests. The Interrogation Centre was in Ham, London, and a lot of the agents were turned (Garbo & Nikolaus Ritter)and acted as double agents rather than being hanged for treason.

German Agents names:

Artist (Johnny Jebsen), Balloon (Dickie Metcalf), Basket (Joseph Lehihan), Beetle (Petur Thomsen), Biscuit (Sam McCarthy), Bootle (Deuxième Bureau), Bronx (Elvira Chaudoir), Brutus (Roman Czerniawski), Careless (Clark Korab), Carrot (? Polish airman), Celery (Walter Dicketts) Charlie (Kiener), Cheese (Renato Levi), Cobweb (Arnason Riis), Dreadnought (Ivan Popov), Dragonfly (Hans George), Father (Henri Arents), Fido (Roger Grosjean), Freak (Marquis Frano de Bona), Gander (Hans Reysen), Garbo (Juan Pujol Garcia), Gelatine (Gerda Sullivan), Gilbert (Andre Latham), Giraffe (Georges Graf), GW (Gwilym Williams), Hamlet (Dr Koestler), Hathchet (Albert de Jaegar), Jacobs (?), Josef (Yuri Smelkov) Le Chat (Mathilde Carré), Lambert (Nikitov), Lipstick (Josef Terradellas), Meteor (Eugn Sostaric), Monoplane (Paul Jeannin), Moonbeam (? Canada), Mullett (Thornton), Mutt & Jeff (Helga Moe & Tor Glad), Peppermint (José Brugada), Puppet (Mr Fanto), Rainbow (Günther Schütz), Rover (?), Scruffy (Alphonse Timmerman), Shepherd (?), The Snark (Maritza Mihailovic), Sniper (?), Snow (Arthur Owens), Spanehl (Ivan Španiel), Spider (?), Springbok (Hans von Kotze), Stephan (Klein), Summer (Gösta Caroli), Sweet William (William Jackson), Tate (Wulf Schmidt), Teapot (?), Treasure (Nathalie Sergueiew), Tricycle (Dušan Popov), Washout (Ernesto Simoes), Watchdog (Werner von Janowski), Weasel (Belgian doctor), The Worm (Stefan Zeiss), Zigzag (Eddie Chapman).

Bletchley Park intercepted Radio Traffic and passed information to MI5.

Nikolaus Ritter   *Admiral Canaris*   *Joan Pujol Garcia*

Radio Room at Abwehr   *Oswald Mosley*

RAF Intelligence, Bletchley Park and Stations Y

Hut 6 - Intelligence Unit

Bletchley Park

Hut 3 - Air Signals

Bletchley Park and Air Ministry Intelligence Unit at Bracknell (40 Officers and 25 Men) & RAF Cheadle played a big role in interpreting German signals through breaking the German codes (Enigma machine). Alan Turing at Bletchley Park and the Air Section at MI6 (A1 C), Wing Commander F.W. Winterbottom picked up German agent traffic.

The Air Ministry Intelligence Section was split up in various departments and worked with MI5 and MI6 –DD14 (Low Countries), DD13 (Luftwaffe Supplies), DD13 (Germany). DD13 was the most important section for the Battle of Britain and was split further A13(D) -Airfields, A13(C) - Aircraft Production A13(B) - Order of Battle. RAF Cheadle monitored regularly with other Y listening stations German signals. These were sent to Bletchley Park who then allocated them to the Air Ministry Intelligence sections to determine the traffic. This was then passed to MI5 and MI6 to act upon. The Station Y units were under the code name SIGNIT, and were set up jointly between the Admiralty and the Air Ministry. They had VHF receivers and monitored traffic. Another special unit was set up called Radio Counter Measures Group (RCM) under Wing Commander E.B. Addison, to combat Knickebein signals. All this work helped the RAF fight in the Battle of Britain.

SIGNIT Scarborough

Scarborough Station Y

Arkley View Station Y

Y Stations

Beachy Head, Sussex; Beaumanor Hall, Loughborough; Beeston Hill, Norfolk; Bishops Waltham, Hampshire; Brora, Sutherland; RAF Canterbury; RAF Cheadle; RAF Chicksands; Cromer, Norfolk; Forest Moor, Harrogate; GPO Transatlantic Station, Kembach; Denmark Hill, Camberwell; Met Office Dunstable; Felistowe, Suffolk; Gilnahirk, Belfast; Gorleston, Norfolk; Hall Place, Kent; Harpenden, (No1 Special Wireless Group); Hawlaw, Fife; HMS Flowerdown, Winchester; HMS Forest Moor, Harrogate; Kedleston Hall, Derbyshire; RAF Kingsdown, Kent; RAF Monks Risbrourgh, Bucks; Knockholt, Kent; Markyate, Herts; Newbold Revel, Warwickshire (RAF Secret Intelligence Base); North Walsham, Norfolk; Sandridge, Herts; Saxmundham, Suffolk; Scarbourgh, Yorkshire; Shenley Brook End, Milton Keynes; South Walsham, Norfolk; Southwold, Suffolk; Stockland Bristol, Bridgwater; Stockton-on-Tees, Cleveland; HMS Ventnor, Rew Down, Isle of Wight; RAF Waddington, Lincs; The Old Rectory, Claypit St, Whitchurch, Shropshire; RAF Wick.

German Intelligence Gathering from Luftwaffe Agents
Josef Schmid (nicknamed Beppo) 5th Abteilang

Between January and June 1939 Luftwaffe Intelligence under Joseph Beppo Schmid (5th Abteilang) was ordered by Göring to assess the RAF Air Defences and structure to allow Germany to plan an invasion, the basis of this report helped the Luftwaffe plans and then Directive 16 and Directive 17. The report was called "Studie Blau" or the Blue Study. The Air Power & Economic Capability of the RAF.

The Blue Plan Study
a. Anti Aircraft defences - results 1,194 guns with locations
b. Searchlights results 3,260 lights as above
c. Bombers strength Hamptons 400, Wellingtons 350, Whitley 300, Hudson 100 with locations.
d. Fighter strength 50 squadrons of 18 aircraft / squadron 50% Hurricanes and 50% Spitfires.
e. Airfields - locations and analysis - well maintained.
f. Supplies - All home production, aircraft production 180 per month, fuel, arms, etc.

This study allowed the Luftwaffe to plan their operational orders which came from Directive 16 and Directive 17 in July 1940 as follows. Schmid lied to Göring during the Battle of Britain on what was being achieved.

Führer Directive 16

1. RAF are to be neutralized
2. Invasion shipping lanes are to cleared from mines
3. Both sides of invasion shipping lanes (Alderney to Portland) and (the Dover Straights) are to be sealed with mines to stop Royal Naval attacks
4. Coastal areas must be captured and commanded.
5. Tie down prior to invasion Royal Naval forces and weaken them significantly.

Führer Directive 17

1. The Luftwaffe will neutralise RAF Ground services
2. Destroy all storage and supply facilities
3. Air Operations secondary targets are naval and merchant shipping after air targets.
4. Support Operation sea lion once objectives above have been achieved.

Operation Orders for attacks on London Luftflotte 2

To commence 7th of September 1940. Three attack areas: a) Right KG30; b) Middle KG1; c) Left KG76.

Fighter escorts will be from JAFU 2: Right JG26 for KG30; Middle JG54 for KG1; Left JG27 for KG76

Josef (Beppo) Schmid

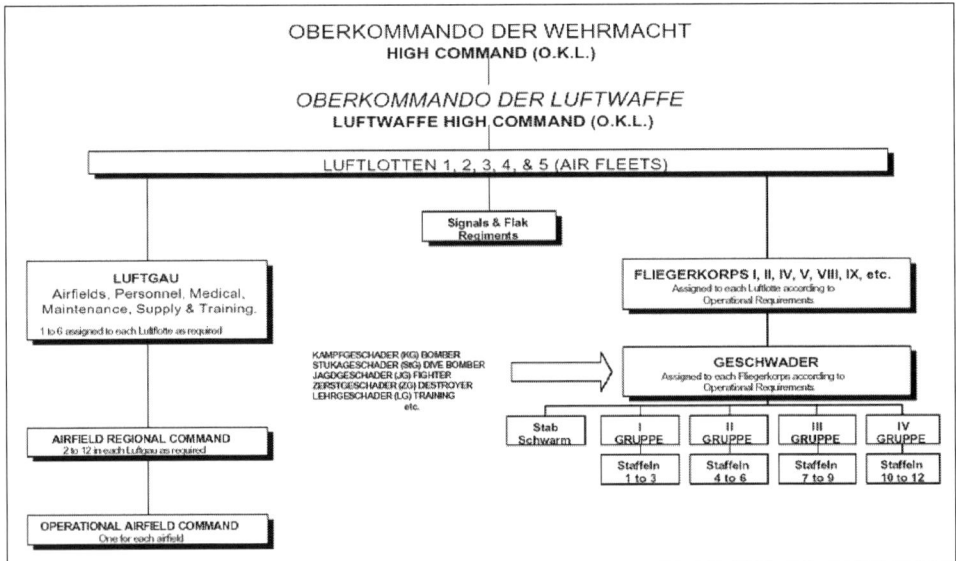

Luftwaffe Organisation

Chapter 7
German Attacks
Timeline: July to October 1940
Summary of Airfields attacked and casualties

The Luftwaffe attack as ordered by Directive 17 was split into 4 phases. The strategy was to suppress air defence and terrorise the population.

Phase 1 - July 10th to August 7th - Attack on shipping - docks and radar stations (Chain Home).

Phase 2 - August 8th to September 6th - Attack on RAF stations - other targets, radar etc. Eagle Day, 13th August, heavy attacks on airfields.

Phase 3 - September 7th to October 5th - London attacks (heavy) and other main cities. September 15th (Battle of Britain Day) major attack on cities; introduction of the RAF Big Wing (12th Group).

Phase 4 - October 6th to 31st October - Attacks on factories and other cities. Heavy attacks on London.

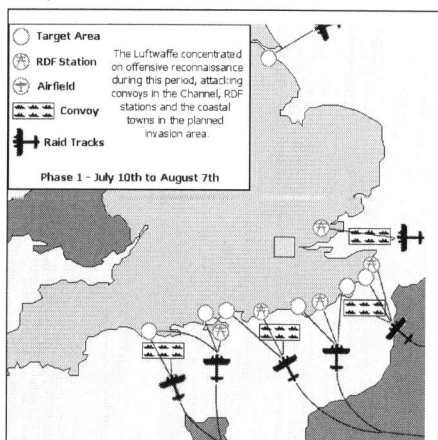

Phase 1

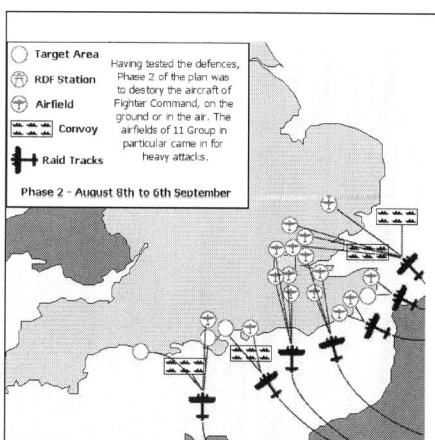

Phase 2

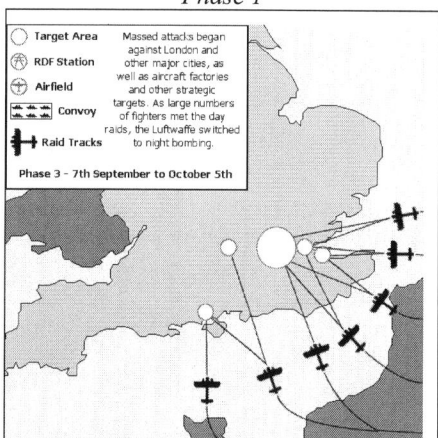

Phase 3

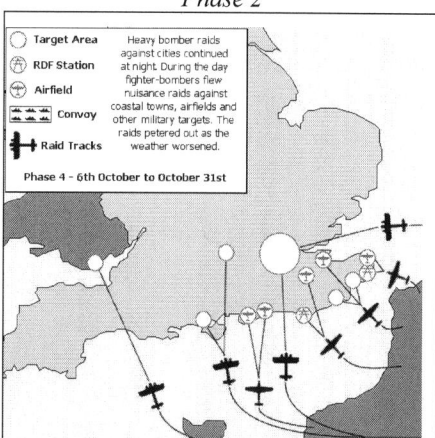

Phase 4

The next few pages list by phase the attacks on Britain by the Luftwaffe and the end pages show the casualties. The raids on the airfield are in the next chapter.

OPERATION SEA LION - Targets identified by Agents 'Snow' - 'Biscuit' and others.

1. Airfields: Sector Airfields, mainly 11, knocked out the Dowding system Chain radar stations and control.
2. Coastal Command stations: anti submarine and shipping, to allow barges for Operation Sea Lion to go unhindered. This included research facilities Gosport and Lee-on-Solent.
3. Ammunition Dumps (Bridlington) and oil terminals - Pembroke Docks, Thames Estuary, Portland Mere Oil Terminal.
4. Aircraft factories, Shorts (Rochester), Spitfire Factory (Castle Bromwich), Rollason factory (Croydon), Vickers factory.
5. Fighter airfields and coastal command fields.

PHASE 1 – July 10th to August 7th – Attacks

July 25th Thursday: Convoy attack Dover Straights Convoy CW8 11 sunk out of 25 plus 2 destroyers- 90xBF109 (Sq Sig1 & Leh2 Calais), attacked by Sq32 & 610 Biggin Hill(1), Sq64 & 615 Kenley(2), Sq54 Rochford(2), Sq111 Croydon and Sq234 St Eval(1). Lost 6 RAF aircraft (attacked by Focke-Wulf 200).

July 26th Friday: Shipping Isle of Wight, Sig77 (Caen) Sq 601 Tangmere, (1), Channel shipping Sq 238 Middle Wallop, Shipping Bristol Channel, Hastings and Weymouth, Aberdeen. Lost 1 RAF aircraft - attacked by Focke-Wulf 200 (Condor).

July 27th Saturday: Attack convoy (codename Bacon) Weymouth, Sq 609 Middle Wallop - no losses.

July 28th Sunday: Attack coast Dover, Rye, Pevensey - from Calais Kg55 60x Heinkels, Leh42 40x Messerschmitts, Sq 41, 74 Hornchurch, 111 Croydon, 257 Northolt. Losses 18 Luftwaffe.

July 29th Monday: Attack Ju87 Stukas x30 (Kg1) and 50x BF109 (Leh2) attacking Dover Sq 64 Kenley Sq 41 Hornchurch (2) RAF lost 2 Luftwaffe 4. Further attack Harwich, He111 & Do17 Sq 66 Coltishall, 17 Debden 85 Mattishall.

July 30th Tuesday: No action.

July 31st Wednesday: Attack on Plymouth by Ju88 (Kg1) Sq 10 RNAS Mountbatten attack in the Channel by Ju87 Sq 74 Hornchurch (2).

Losses for July:

RAF – 33 Hurricanes (23 killed), 34 Spitfires (25), 4 Blenheims (9), 6 Defiant (10), – Total 77.

Luftwaffe – 39 Dornier DO17 (30), 32 Heinkel 111 (52), 39 Junkers 88 (52), 12 Junkers 87 (10), 48 BF109 (17), 18 Bf1 110 (13), other (27), destroyed (19) Total 216.

August 1st Thursday: Photo Recon Cherburg Sq 59 Blenheims Thorney Island and Sq 236 (2), escorts, convoys attacked Yorkshire (Agent & Arena) and Boulton Paul factory, Sq 616 & 607 intercepts, attack in the Channel Sq 145 (1) intercepts.

August 2nd Friday: Raids Forth Bridge shipping, Harwich and Christchurch air raid, Sq 65 (1), Sq 66 (1).

August 3rd Saturday: Fog.

August 4th Sunday: No incidents No 616 1 lost.

August 5th Monday: Attack British shipping in the Channel (Kag54) 30x BF109s over Dover intercepted by Sq 41 Hornchurch, Sq 151 North Weald, Sq 64 (1) Kenley, and Sq 65 (1).

August 6th Tuesday: Strong winds. Lost Sq 17 (1), Sq 72 (1), Sq 234 (1).

August 7th Wednesday: Luftwaffe planning attacks, convoy attacked Cromer Sq 616 (1).

August 8th Thursday: Still planning Eagle Day - Convoy CW9 (Peewit) Southend to Swanage attacked by Luftwaffe Kg27 Tours, Sq 41, Sq 64, Sq 65 (2), Sq 257 (3), Sq 43 (2), Sq145 (5), attacked 70 BF109 (Kag3) & Me110 (Leh2), Sq 238 (2).

August 9th Friday: Bad weather lost 1 aircraft Sq 605 Drem, Scotland. (Mountbatten attacked) Sq 600 (1), Sq 605 (1).

Junker 87 Stukas in convoy

Convoy 14th July 1940

Ship on fire in English Channel (1940)

Convoys 1940

PHASE 2 – Sunday 11th August to September 6th
including Adlertag (Eagle Day)

10th August Saturday: - RAF West Malling, Norwich, Midlands

11th August Sunday: - Portland Naval Base, Dover, Rochford 30x BF110 (from Leh 1) and from Kg27 20x Heinkel He111 and from Leh1 Zg2 30x BF109s: Total 170 German aircraft - Sq1 (1), Sq17 (1), Sq56 (1), Sq74 (2), Sq87 (1), Sq111(4), Sq145 (2), Sq152 (1), Sq213 (2), Sq238 (4), Sq601 (3), Sq609, 610 (2): Losses Luftwaffe (38) RAF (32)

12th August Monday: -Raid on Portsmouth, Lee, 5 RAF Fields Hawkinge & Lympne unservicable, Manston, Rochford, Hornchurch- Radar Stations CHL, Dover, Dunkirk, Foreland, Pevensey, Poling, Rye, Ventnor, Sq54 , Sq65, Sq145 (3), Sq213 (2), Sq257 (1), Sq266 (1), Sq501 (1) by Eppro210 Kg51, Zg2, Zg76 and Jg53 aircraft. Losses Luftwaffe (31) RAF (22).

13th August Tuesday:- **Aldertag (Eagle Day)**- Strong formation to attack **06:45** RAF stations in England. Kg2 74x Dorniers, Zer26 60x BF110 Sq43 Tangmere, Sq64 Kenley, Sq65 Hornchurch (1), Sq 87 Filton (1), Sq601 Tangmere, Ju88 from Kg54 bomb Royal Aircraft Establishments Odiham & Farnborough, RAF Benson, Middle Wallop. **07:20** Sq74, Sq111, Croydon, Sq151 North Weald attack on RAF Eastchurch & Sheerness by Kg2 Dorniers Do17, and Ju88s of Kg54. **11:40** Portland Harbour and RAF Thorney Island Sq238 and Sq601 attacked Bf110 from Zg2, 1500 RAF Tangmere & Westhampnett defended by Sq152, Sq213 (1), Sq238 (1), Sq609 KG54 40x BF109, 77xJu87, Sig77 and Sig2 escorts, 50x BF109. 1700 Attack on Shorts Rochester factory, RAF Detling, Aircraft factories also, Belfast, Castle Bromwich, Aberdeen, Liverpool. Losses RAF 13 Luftwaffe 34. Full Targets - RAF Biggin Hill (Kg1), RAF Kenley, Debden, Biggin Hill (Kg76), RAF Hornchurch, Eastchurch & Manston (Kg2), RAF Eastchurch (Kg3), RAF North Weald (Kg53), RAF Hawkinge, Manston, Kenley, Radar Rye, Pevensey, Dover, (Erprobungsgruppe 210), RAF Dishforth (Kg40, 26), RAF Linton (Kg26), RAF Driffield (Kg30), Ports of Bristol, Birkenhead, Liverpool (Kg27), RAF Worthy Down, Detling ports of Southampton, Portsmouth, Lee (Leh1), RAF Bibury, Spithead, Ventnor Radar (Kg51), Fleet Air Arm Gosport, RAF Croydon, Odiham, Farnborough (Kg54), Fleet Air Arm Plymouth, RAF Feltham, Middle Wallop (Kg55), RAF Warmwell & Detling (Sig1), Portland area, RNAS Yeovilton, RAF Middle Wallop, Feltham (Sig2), RAF Warmwell & Portland Area (Sig77)

14th August Wednesday:-Kg3 & Jag26 RAF airfields Manston, Sealand, Middle Wallop attacks Cardiff, Folkestone, Dover Andover - Goodwin lightship sank - Kg3 BF110 and Jg26 & Jg52 Lost Luftwaffe 21 RAF 6, defence Sq32 (1), Sq43 (1), Sq151 (1), Sq609 (1) Sq615 (2).

15th **August (Black Thursday):** - Attacks 72x Kg26 He111, Zg76 21x BF110 RAF Airfields Croydon. **18:50** Portland & South Coast Kg2 attack Dorniers Sq111 caught in the middle of the attack but took off, Middle Wallop. **17:50** 40x BF110, 60x JU88 from LG1, West Malling. 18:50 Kg3 attack Sq32 scrambled, Eastchurch, Martlesham Heath, Kg3 16x BF110, Ju87 and BF109, Hawkinge, Lympne, attack on Short Brothers factory in Rochester. From 60x BF109 (Leh2), 25x BF110, 40x Ju87 and Dishford, Linton on Ouse, Usworth and Bridlington ammunition dump attacked by 34x Me110, Norway 50x Ju88 (Kg30) from Denmark blown up. Defence No1 (2), Sq72, Sq54, Sq64,(2), Sq151 (2), Sq501, Sq87 (2), Sq111 (1), Sq213 (1), Sq609, Sq234 (2), Sq266 (2), Sq615 (1). Losses RAF Luftwaffe.

16th **August Friday:** RAF Biggin Hill, Kenley, Croydon and Northolt, other targets, Manston,West Malling, Tangmere, Gosport, Lee on Solent **13:00** 20x Ju87 (7 killed), Farnborough and Harwell, Ventnor Radar then Middle Wallop, Brize Norton (much damage), also Harrow, Lee, Wealdstone, Malden, Wimbledon, Gravesend & Tilbury. Losses Luftwaffe 44, RAF 28.

17th **August Saturday:** - Night raids over the Midlands, Merseyside and South Wales. Losses Luftwaffe 3, RAF 1. Sq235 (1)

18th **August Sunday:** - Poling Radar station RAF airfields Croydon, Kenley West Malling and Ford (all badly damaged), Gosport and Thorney Island attacked, factory in Croydon, Rollason factory- defended by Sq152, Sq601, Sq602, Sq234. Losses Luftwaffe 69 RAF 43.

19th **August Monday:** - Fliegerkorps 8 attacked Pembroke Dock. Losses Luftwaffe 10, RAF 5. Sq1(1), Sq66 (1), Sq92 (1), Sq248 (3), Sq602 (1).

20th **August Tuesday:** Attacks on RAF West Malling, Eastchurch, Manston, Losses Luftwaffe 8 RAF 2. Sq65 (1), Sq242 (1). Sig1, and Sig77 (Ju87s) and AU11 (Dorniers plus Jag57).

21st **August Wednesday:** - Light attack St Eval Sq56 (1). Losses Luftwaffe 13, RAF 1.

22nd **August Thursday:** - Light attacks St Eval, Wick, Manston, North Weald-Sq54 (1), Sq65 (1), Sq610 (1), Sq 616 (1). Losses Luftwaffe 4, RAF 5.

23rd **August Friday:** London attack also South Wales, Cardiff, Pembroke Luftwaffe 5, RAF 1, Sq1 (1).

24th **August Saturday:** - RAF Manston completely destroyed other airfields Hornchurch and North Weald, attack on London, Losses Luftwaffe 38 RAF 22.

25th August Sunday: Attacks Dorset coast, Thames estuary, Birmingham, Coventry, Reading, South Wales, Scotland. Luftwaffe 20, RAF 16.

26th August Monday: Kg3 RAF attacks Debden North Weald, Hornchurch Kg2 RAF Biggin Hill & Kenley Sq43 losses Luftwaffe 41, RAF 31. Night attacks Coventry, Bournemouth, Plymouth.

27th August Tuesday: Attacks on Factories. Losses Luftwaffe 7, RAF 4.

28th August Wednesday: Attacks on RAF Rochford & Eastchurch, Midland cities plus heavy raid on London. Losses Luftwaffe 31, RAF 17.

29th August Thursday: Luftlotte 2 fighter sweeps over Kent no contact, Liverpool attacked. Losses Luftwaffe 17, RAF 10.

30th August Friday: RAF Biggin Hill (severely damaged). Attacks also on Kenley, North Weald, Northolt, Slough, Oxford and also RAF Detling, Shoreham and Tangmere. Losses Luftwaffe 36, RAF 25.

31st August Saturday: RAF Croydon, Debden, Biggin Hill, Hornchurch, North Weald, Duxford & Eastchurch, Sq264 & Sq141. Losses Luftwaffe 41, RAF 41.

1st September Sunday: Biggin Hill (armoury set ablaze), Detling, Eastchurch, Lympne, Hawkinge. Night attacks on Liverpool & South Wales. Losses Luftwaffe 14, RAF 14.

2nd September Monday: Biggin Hill, Detling, Hornchurch, Eastchurch. Night raids on Liverpool, Midlands, East Anglia and South West. Losses Luftwaffe 35, RAF 17.

3rd September Tuesday: RAF Debden, Hornchurch, North Weald (badly damaged) attacked. Night raids on Liverpool, South East & South Wales. Losses Luftwaffe 16, RAF 16.

4th September Wednesday: RAF Eastchurch attacked and also airfields producing aircraft Vickers at Brookland, Shorts at Rochester, Kingston, Langley and Southampton, also Canterbury, Faversham, Reigate. Losses Luftwaffe 25, RAF 16.

5th September Thursday: RAF Biggin Hill, Detling, Croydon, North Weald, Lympne, and oil tanks at Thameshaven. Losses Luftwaffe 23, RAF 19.

6th September Friday: Hawker factory at Weybridge, oil tanks at Thameshaven. Losses Luftwaffe 35, RAF 21.

7th September Saturday: RAF Hawkinge. Luftwaffe 41, RAF 26. Luftwaffe directed by the Fuhrer to switch attacks on London.

Stage 3 and Stage 4 will be the subject of further material and publications.

Aircraft Losses July to October 1940
Shot down (air) and ground attack

MONTH	LUFT-WAFFE	RAF	TOTAL
July	216	77	293
August	774	426	1,200
September	696	248	573
October	291	336	627
Total	1,977	1,087	3,064
Aircraft Available	2,953	1,796	

Luftwaffe Stats for August (losses)

Me109 - 229; Me110 -123; DO17 - 75; He111 - 98; Ju88 - 104; Ju87 - 62; Other - 83; Total - 774.

Pilots Killed - 216; Captured - 13; Missing - 264; Rescued - 281; Total - 774.

RAF Pilots

COUNTRY	NO.	KIA
British & Commonwealth	1,822	339
Fleet Air Arm	56	9
Australian	21	14
New Zealanders	73	11
Canadian	88	20
South African	21	9
Rhodesian	2	0
American	7	1
Polish	141	29
Czech	86	8
Belgian	26	6
Free French	13	0
Israeli	1	0
Total	2,365	446

Civilians July to December 1940
Deaths: 23,003 Wounded: 32,138

PHASE 3 Air Attacks on Towns

Air Attacks on Swansea *(for the benefit of the Welsh lads from South Wales in the Oxford Welsh Male Voice Choir - Y Tangnefeddwyr)*

Here I show what the British people had to suffer from the Luftwaffe onslaught and how terrifying the attacks were. Swansea was a port in Wales that was used to receive food supplies and arms from the World and North America, it was a target for the Luftwaffe. The town had 500 communal air shelters as well as Anderson shelters. There were anti-aircraft gun defences near the docks.

Swansea Air Attacks

The first attack was at 03:30 hrs on the 27th of June 1940, a marker flare was dropped, then there followed bombers with high explosives targeting the docks. Bombs hit Danygrig residential area. There were some unexploded ordnance in the Kilvey Hill area. There were also single bomber raids during the rest of 1940 and a small scale raid in January 1941. However the worst raid was on the nights of the 19th, 20th and 21st of February 1941. The first raid started at 19:30 hrs on the 19th.

On the 19th the Regimental Headquarters of the 79th Hertfordshire Yeoman-ry Heavy Anti-Aircraft Regiment was hit and the Operations room was destroyed. Two officers were killed and 5 other ranks. On the 21st RAF Pembrey was attacked (Ops Room); there was now no protection for Swansea (No92 Squadron was moved on the 12th August 1940). As a result the centre of Swansea was devastated, 230 were killed and 409 injured. 7,000 people lost their homes, many commercial premises were destroyed, with Ben Evans department store, the Victorian market. 14 hours of bombing, 1,273 high explosive bombs dropped and 56,000 incendiaries, 857 homes were completely destroyed and 11,000 damaged. There was another raid on the 16th February 1943. Target information was sent by agent "Snow" to the German Abwehr and gun emplacements knocked out.

16c Swansea school bombed

Swansea blitz 1940 (Owens Store)

Britain's Home Front 1939-45

Winston Churchill visiting air raid damage.

Monument to the Air Defence, Swansea

War-time total destruction

Chapter 8
RAF Airfield Attacks
(Details of the large raids only)

AIRFIELD	№	DATES	AIRFIELD	№	DATES
Andover	1	August 14	**Manston**	7	Aug 12, 14, 16, 18, 20, 22, 25
Benson	1	August 13			
Bibury	1	August 13	**Middle Wallop**	4	August 13, 14, 15, 16
Biggin Hill	7	Aug 13, 16 26, 30, 31. Sept 1, 6	Martlesham Heath	1	August 15
Brize Norton	1	August 16	**North Weald**	8	Aug 13, 22, 24, 26, 30, 31, Sept 3, 5
Cardiff	1	August 14			
Croydon	6	August 13, 15, 16, 19, 27, Sept 2	Northolt	1	August 30
			Oxford	1	August 30
Dishforth, Driffield	1	August 13	Odiham	1	August 13
			Pembroke Docks	4	July 28, Aug 19, 23, 24, Sept 1
Debden	4	August 15, 26, 31, Sept 3			
Detling	5	Aug 11, 13, 30, Sept 1, 2, 5	Plymouth (Mountbatten	1	August 13
Duxford	1	August 31	**Portland**	4	July 4, August 11, 13, 15
Eastchurch	8	Aug 13, 15, 20, 28, 31, Sept 4, 5	**Rochford**	4	August 12, 26, 28, 30
			Sealand	1	August 14
Folkestone	1	August 13	Shoreham	1	August 30
Farnborough	1	August 14	Slough	1	August 30
Feltham	1	August 16	**St Eval**	6	August 21, 22, 23, 26, Sept 30, Oct
Ford	1	August 18			
Gosport	3	August 12, 16, 18	**Tangmere**	3	August 13, 16, 30
Hawkinge	6	Aug 12, 13, 15, Sept 1, 2, 5	**Thorney Island**	4	August 13, 16, 18, 23
Harwell	1	August 16	Yeovilton	1	August 13
Hornchurch	6	August 13, 24, 26, 31, Sept 2, 3	Warmwell	1	August 13
Kenley	6	August 13, 15, 16, 18, 26, Sept 1	**West Malling**	6	Aug 15, 16, 18, 21, 24, Sept 3
Lympne	5	August 12, 15, 30, Sept 1, 5	Westhampnett	1	August 13
			Witney	1	August 18
Lee on Solent	3	August 12, 13, 16			

Chain Home Radar Stations:
Pevensey, Rye, Dover, Dunkirk, Poling, Foreland, Ventnor - Aug 12; Poling - Aug 16 to18.

Cities attacked (Ports):
Bristol - Aug 18, 24, 25; Cardiff - Aug 23; Liverpool - Aug 7, 28, 29, Sept 2, 5; Portsmouth - Aug 24, 27, Sept 11; Plymouth - Aug 9; Southampton - Aug 24, Sept 4, 11.

RAF BIGGIN HILL (call sign SAPPER) 'Sector C' HQ
Commander: Wing Commander Richard Grice

Museums: Biggin Hill Memorial Tel 01959-422414 or Spitfire 01959-576767
Email: office@bigginhillspitfire.com Biggin Hill Air Show – 01959-578500

Biggin Hill Civil Airport   *Biggin Hill from the air*

Units on the Airfield in the Battle of Britain

Spitfires: Sq72 and Sq74 (moved to Hornchurch), Sq92 and Sq610
Hurricanes: Sq32 (moved to Acklington), Sq43 (moved from Tangmere),
Sq79 (moved from Pembrey) and Sq242 (moved to Coltishall), and Sq501
(moved from Croydon) and Defiants: Sq141 (moved to West Malling). The
Anti-Aircraft Defence School was also on the airfield.

Air Attacks:

August 13th - attack by KG1 and KG76 - damage to airfield, attacked married quarters at Vincent Square. August 16th (13:00) some damage.
August 18th - by KG76 - Dornier DO17s and Ju88s - cratered the runways
some building damage. **August 30th** (18:00) 2 attacks on the same day - 12x
1000lbs bombs 9x JU88, blew up workshops, stores, barracks, guardroom,
WAAF quarters and hangers - killed 39 personnel. 3 WAAF received the
Military Medal Corporal Elspeth Henderson, Sergeant Elizabeth Mortimer,
and Sergeant Helen Turner. **August 31st** (17:30) Operations Room was
destroyed and suffered a direct hit. Hangers North & South Camp.
September 1st - two attacks, on the second attack blew up the sector operations room, blew up the ammunition store, only one squadron was able to
operate from the airfield, the rest were moved. Headquarters moved to
Keston House 3 miles away. WAAF Station Officer Hanbury received the
Military Medal. **September 1st** (13:30) - building damage, 1 aircraft destroyed, communication and fuel line hit, 3 craters. **September 6th** - damage
to dispersal area, main runway and telephone lines. No casualties.

RAF BIGGIN HILL RECORDS AIR28/64	OFFICERS	AIRMEN	CIVILIANS	TOTAL	KILLED
Commandant Wing Commander Richard Grice	3	6		9	
Headquarters Staff	30	510	30	570	39
WAAF Station Officer F Hanbury	3	200		203	
Sub Total Head Quarters staff	**36**	**716**	**30**	**782**	**39**
Airfield Defences 5 gun emplacements					
88th AA Brigade	**10**	**200**		**210**	
30th Surrey Searchlight Brigade	**2**	**100**		**102**	
904th A Flight Barrage Balloons	**2**	**100**		**102**	
Royal Engineers					
Observer Corps					
No22 Barrage Balloon Storage Unit					
Sub Total non air crew	**4**	**200**	**30**	**234**	
Total Station (Air crew muster)	**54**	**1,316**	**60**	**1,430**	**39**
Anti Aircraft Defence School					
Squadron including pilots per squadron - 10 squadrons	(varied due to extensive movements)				
Squadrons 32, 43, 72, 74, 79, 92, 141, 242, 501, 610	181	480		661	39

Squadron scramble

Servicing a Hurricane

Downed Dornier at Biggin Hill

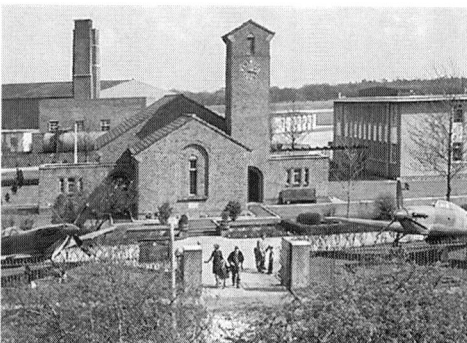

Biggin Hill buildings

Biggin Hill RAF Fighter Command

Squadron 612 at Biggin Hill

Winston Churchill visits Biggin Hill

Biggin Hill Chapel (Spitfire 2)

Biggin Hill Officers Mess

Belgian ground crew refuelling a Spitfire

Biggin Hill damage - living quarters

Biggin Hill - WAAF Military Medals

RAF CROYDON 'Sector B' Subsidiary to RAF Kenley
Commander: Wing Commander T.B. Prickman

Airport Museum, Purley Way, Croydon, CR0 0XZ
Tel: 0208-680-5878 Email: cas.cave@hotmail.co.uk

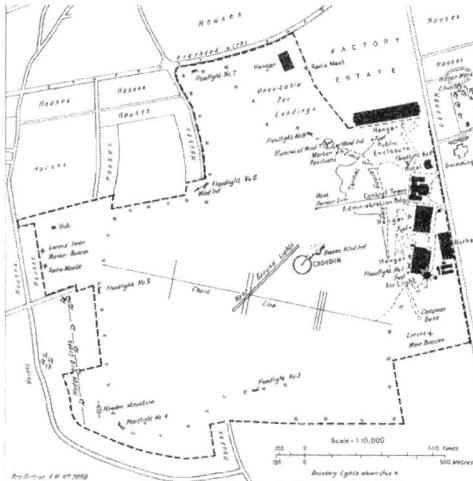

Croydon Airfield 1940   *Croydon Airport 1945*

Units on the Airfield in the Battle of Britain:

Sq1 RCAF (moved to Northolt), Sq3 (moved to Manston), Sq17(to Debden), Sq32 (moved to Biggin Hill), Sq72 - Gladiators, Sq85 (moved to Debden), Sq111 - Hurricanes, Sq350 (Belgium)-Hurricanes, Sq605-Hurricane.

The airfield stored fuel and ammunition, together with accommodation for pilots.

Air Attacks

August 13th (13:00) attack by KG54 & KG27 (JU88s supported by BF109s) damage.

August 15th (18:20) KUL26 -2x Heinkels and BF109 destroyed the armoury, passenger terminal building, A & D hangers there were 7 killed (5x Sq111, 1x Sq1 1x WAAF in the control (telephones), also the Rollason Aircraft factory and Bourjois Perfume factory were attacked - 62 killed and 192 wounded.

August 19th - (13:25) attacked Heinkels & Dorniers He11& He8 delayed bombs. A Hanger destroyed, 2 large craters in runway, hit main building, guard room, 11 injured.

August 27th -(01:32) attacked by KG2 1x Heinkel destroyed 1 Hurricane, hit 2 gun Posts №1 & №7 no injury.

September 2nd - (12:55) 12 aircraft B Hanger damaged, cookhouse shot up, lorry blown up.

RAF CROYDON RECORDS AIR28/178	OFFICERS	AIRMEN	CIVILIANS	TOTAL	KILLED
Headquarters Staff (estimated)					
Headquarters Staff	30	400	30	460	
WAAF	3	60		63	69
Sub Total Head Quarters staff	**33**	**460**	**30**	**523**	**69**
Airfield Defences Anti-Aircraft Units					
148th Battery - 12 emplacements					
27th AA Brigade (Brigadier A.B. Ogle)	20	400		420	
30th Searchlight Brigade					
"D" Company 8th Middlesex					
"D" Company 2nd Battalion Tower Hamlets	4	200		204	
Royal Engineers					
Balloons Units					
Observer Corp	2	100		102	
Sub Total	**59**	**1,160**		**1,219**	
RAF Squadrons					
Sq1 RCAF, Sq3, Sq17, Sq32, Sq72, Sq85, Sq111, Sq350, Sq605					
Total Air Crew	**90**	**432**		**522**	
Total Number on Station	**149**	**1,592**		**1,741**	**69**

Hurricane bought by Croydon residents

Croydon Airport bomb damage

Croydon Airport - awaiting the bombs

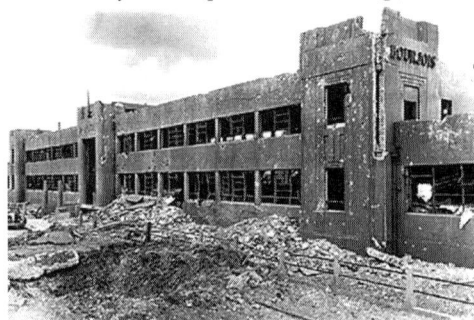
Bourjois Perfume Factory, Croydon

RAF DEBDEN (Call Sign GARTER) HQ 'Sector E'
Wing Commander Laurence Fuller-Good
Taken over by the USAF in 1941

RAF Debden Airfield

Top Right: Station Area
Right: Debden Fighter Pilots

Units on the Airfield in the Battle of Britain:

Sq17 Hurricane, Sq29 Blenheims, Sq85 Hurricane and Sq257 (moved to Northolt), Sq1 moved to Northolt, Sq65 moved to Hornchurch, Sq80 ?, Sq87 moved to Filton, Sq111 moved to Croydon, Sq157 ?, Sq257 moved to Northolt, Sq 418 ?,Sq517 moved to Filton, Sq601 moved to Tangmere.

August 2nd - Heavy attack destroyed several buildings.

August 11th (12:16) - squadron scramble saw off attack.

August 15th (07:00) KG76 & KG2 300 aircraft with ZC26 dropped 20 HE Bombs by 1x DO17 - no severe damage. Hit two wooden huts and guard room, 3 injured.

August 26th (15:19) KG3 100 H5 incendiary bombs, destroyed Airman's quarters, NAAFI Sergeants' mess direct hits, and damaged WAAF quarters, Motor Transport Pool. Equipment building was seriously damaged. 4 RAF killed and 1 civilian.

August 31st - Sergeants' mess and NAAFI badly damaged.

September 5th - after air attacks, HQ building moved to a grammar school at Saffron Walden.

RAF DEBDEN RECORDS AIR28/187	OFFICERS	AIRMEN	CIVILIANS	TOTAL	KILLED
Headquarters Staff (estimated)					
Headquarters Staff	26	365	30	421	5
WAAF	3	60		36	
Sub Total	**29**	**425**	**30**	**484**	**5**
Airfield Defences Anti-Aircraft Units (4 emplacements)					
41st AA Brigade	8	400		408	
30th Searchlights	2	100		102	
904th Balloon 'B' Flight	2	100		102	
Royal Engineers					
Observer Corp	2	100		102	
Sub Total	**43**	**1,125**	**30**	**1,198**	**5**
Total Ground Crew					
RAF Squadrons					
Sq1, Sq29, Sq65, Sq80, Sq157, Sq257, Sq418					
Total Air Crew	**70**	**336**		**406**	
Total Number on Station	**113**	**1,461**	**30**	**1,604**	

Entrance to RAF Debden

Debden Airfield - Hurricane

Duchess of Kent visits RAF Debden

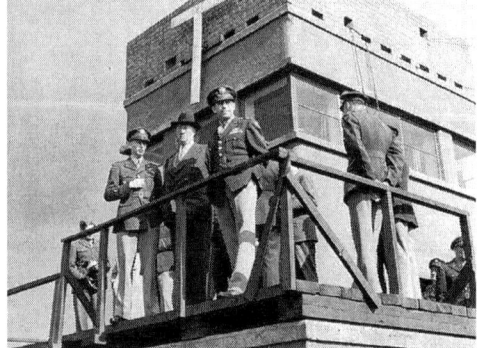
RAF Debden Control Tower

RAF DETLING 'Sector B' Kent County Show Ground
Group Captain Edward Davis (KIA 13th August)
Followed by G.Capt. F.L. Hopps.

Detling airfield

Detling airfield (1946)

Units on the Airfield in the Battle of Britain:

Sq 500 Avro Ansons, Sq 53, Sq 235 (moved 10th June) Bristol Blenheims, Sq 1 Coastal Artillery Group and Sq 4 Lysanders, Sq 266.

Air Raids

August 13th (16:00) - worst air attack on any RAF airbase ever: JAG26 - 40x BF109; KG54 - 77x JU88; SIG1 - 40x JU87 (Stukas). Severe damage to runways, destroyed all hangers and Operations Room, killed Group Captain Edward Davis. 22 RAF aircraft were destroyed as well as WAAF quarters and mess hall at Friningham Manor, 68 killed officially (at least 3 civilian deaths but records should have more as they were not recorded in the attack, and also those manning Bofors anti-aircraft guns). The WAAFs were moved to Binbury Manor. Two military medals were awarded: WAAF Sgt Mary Youle and Cpl Jessie Robins. **August 30th** High level attack, 5 Blenheims of 53 squadron destroyed. **September 1st** - Attack set the Officers Mess on fire. **September 2nd** - Attack put out of action for 3 hours, high flying Dornier DO17S. **September 5th** (15:55) 20 Me109s dive bombed Gun Battery 337 at Hartlip. Shot down 1 intruder.

The Fateful Day - August 13th

On August 13th there was a massive attack on RAF Detling. Aircraft were on the airfield fuelled and armed that day ready for Operations that evening before the attack when 88 were killed. The bodies of the RAF Squadrons were taken to Preston Hall Hospital in Aylesford and the body parts and non RAF personnel (WAAFs) taken under armed escort by the 2nd/5th East

Surrey Home Guard 27 truck convoy to the Royal Naval Hospital, Chatham for identification and burial. The records have disapperaed.

A witness to the WAAF body parts, Albert Bartholomew, who used an excavator: "One day it was really bad, a lot of WAAFs were killed over in the Ops Room (opposite the showground entrance), I had to dig a trench to bury them, they were under a tarpaulin, all arms and legs just jumbled up, men and women". The AIR81 records have disappeared, but we think we have found all the names now in the Hospital records.

RAF DETLING RECORDS AIR28/187	OFFICERS	RAF	WAAF	CIVILIANS	TOTAL	KILLED
Headquarters Staff						
Commandant Wing Co	2	17			17	4
Admin & Accounts	1	5			6	4
Armourers	1	50			51	
Communications - Telephones	1	40	10		51	
Catering & Mess	2	45	13		60	
Maintenance	1	40		12	53	
Operations Room	13	6	12		31	31
Personnel & Records	1	2	4		7	6
Stores & Equipment	3	60	10	10	83	
Transport & Drivers	3	60	10	10	83	1
Workshops	2	50		2	54	2
Sub Total	**30**	**375**	**59**	**34**	**498**	**48**
Airfield Defences Anti-Aircraft Units 2nd/5th East Surrey Reg.	Heavy Anti Aircraft Batteries - Fort Luton - Chatham 28th HAA Brigade; S3- 207/58th HAA and S4- 234/89th HAA					
268.67 Battery						1
265.67 Battery	4	106			110	2
256.67 Battery	5	117			122	2
Royal Engineers						
RE 703	1	67			68	3
RE 513 - 1 observer searchlight	0	7			7	1
AA 53	2	40			42	1
Balloon 961st A Flight 15 balloons	2	40			42	
Observer 26th Kent Searchlight	2	40	5		47	5
Sub Total	**46**	**792**	**64**	**34**	**936**	**62**
RAF Squadrons						
Squadron 53	29	451			480	20*
Squadron 500	41	382			423	5
Other Units	7	401			408	
Sub Total	**77**	**1,234**			**1,311**	**22**
Total Airfield Headcount	**123**	**2,026**	**64**	**34**	**2,247**	**88**

* includes 3 civilians

RAF Detling - 13th August 1940 - AIR RAID

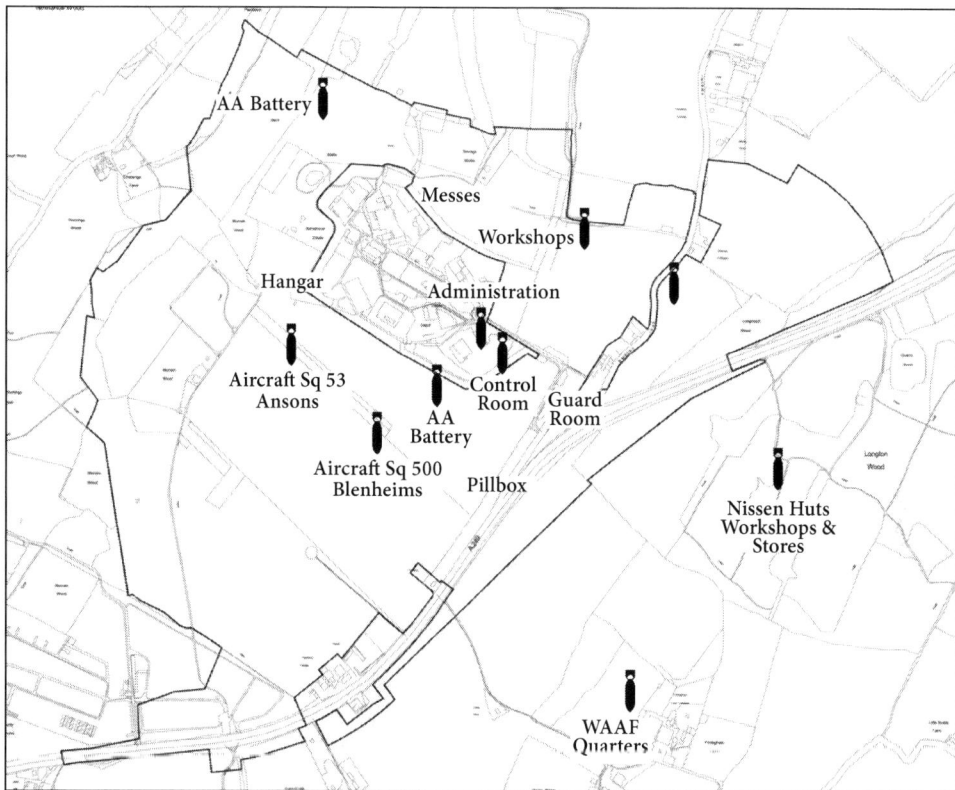

AA Battery

Messes

Workshops

Hangar

Administration

Aircraft Sq 53
Ansons

Control
Room

Guard
Room

AA
Battery

Aircraft Sq 500
Blenheims

Pillbox

Nissen Huts
Workshops &
Stores

WAAF
Quarters

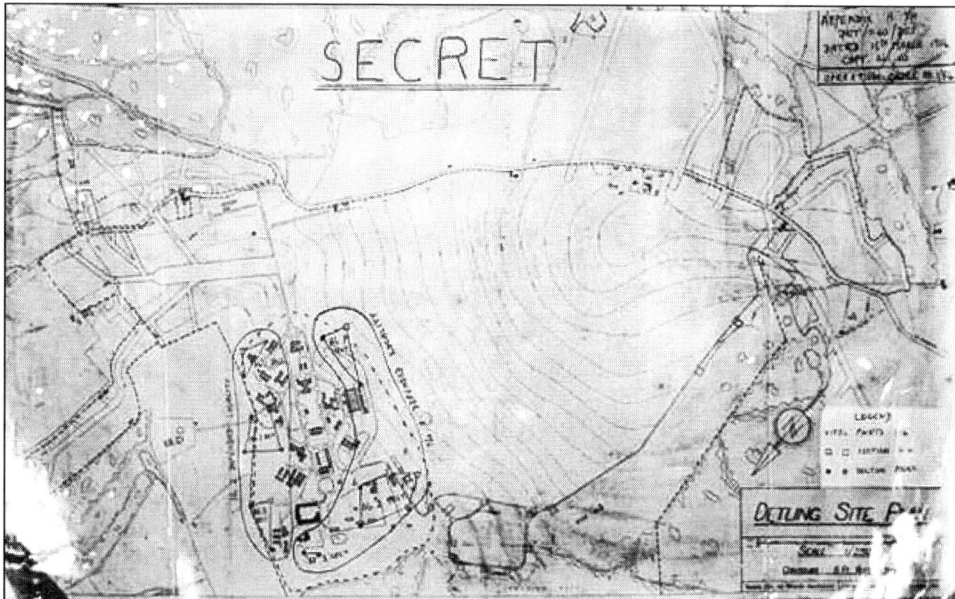

RAF Detling Airfield Secret Site Plan

RAF Detling Airfield and Buildings - 1943

National Archive Record:

After an initial existence as a defensive fighter station from 3 April 1917 to 31 October 1919, Detling re-opened as an Expansion Scheme station on 14 September 1938 in No 6 (Auxiliary) Group of Bomber Command, accommodating No 500 Squadron converted to Ansons.

From the outbreak of war the squadron carried out convoy protection patrols until things hotted-up in May 1940 when it, and other squadrons using Detling, became involved in covering the Dunkirk evacuation. On 30 May 1940 WAAF Cpl Daphne Pearson won the Empire Gallantry Medal for her part in rescuing the pilot of a crashed Anson (See Reply of 25 February 2011).

Detling suffered a devastating attack on 13 August 1940, mentioned earlier in this thread; all the hangars were wrecked with most of the technical and domestic buildings, plus 22 aircraft. 57 RAF and civilian staff were killed, including the Station CO, and 94 injured. Many of the casualties were local men from 500 Squadron. There were further attacks on 30 August and 2 September. The pilot of a No 111 Squadron Hurricane force landed on the airfield with engine failure at the height of the latter raid – he was recorded as being "not a happy man"! Two WAAFs received the Military Medal for remaining at their posts throughout the attack.

After the Battle of Britain Detling became something of a backwater, its only occupants being the RAF Regiment after 500 Squadron moved out in May

1941. It first transferred to Fighter Command, who made little use of it, then to Army Cooperation Command on 1 January 1943. Despite being just a small grass airfield, a USAAF B-17 with 2 engines 'out' made a successful landing on 9 October 1942. The station almost had a mutiny on its hands in March 1943 when No 318 (Polish) Squadron formed a reconnaissance unit with obsolete Hurricanes and the Poles were recorded as being "a very unhappy bunch"!

RAF Detling Air Raid 13/08/1940 – Deaths

Ref	Orig Ref	Airfield	Title	Surname	First Names	DoB	Serial	Rank	Squad-ron	Buried
1	1	Detling OB	Mr	Aspen	Harold Milne		35328	Flying Officer	53	Hadenham
2	2	Detling	Mr	Bateman	William Frank		563962	Corporal	53	Maidstone
3	3	Detling	Mr	Bishop	Leslie George		1989620	Sapper 703 RE		Maidstone
4	4	Detling	Mr	Booth	George		943762	AC1	53	Huddersfield
5	6	Detling	Mr	Brereton	Joseph Patrick		997958	AC2	53	Manchester
6	7	Detling	Mr	Brooker	Albert Frederick		1168029	AC2	53	Maidstone plot 95
7	8	Detling	Mr	Brookes	Leonard Edwin	07/07/1913	573086	AC1 Fitter DFC	53	Maidstone plot 100
8	40	DoW	Mr	Butler	Dennis William		759274	Sergeant Obs		Andover
9	9	Detling	Mr	Cassely	Albert Harold	06/10/1896	13633	Corporal	53	Heston
10	10	Detling	Mr	Collerton	William		526331	LAC	53	Maidstone plot 98
11	11	Detling	Mr	Crote	William James	12/03/1913	1010974	AC2	53	Bream
12	12	Detling	Mr	Dancaster	Arthur Frank	16/08/1919	567998	LAC Fitter 2	53	Maidstone
13	13	Detling	Mr	Davies	Wilfred Eric		81970	Pilot Officer	53	Maidstone
14	14	Detling OB	Mr	Davis	Edward Peverel		2893211	Group Captain	53	KIA Ops Room
15	15	Detling	Mr	Deeley	George	01/06/1903	328721	Corporal		Selly Oak
16	16	Detling	Mr	Francis	Joseph		1550619	Gunner 265/67		Maidstone
17	17	Detling	Mr	Heath	Reginald H George		1550631	Searchlight 569		Maidstone
18	41	DoW	Mr	Hill	Leonard Charles		956258	Sergeant		Montrose
19	18	Detling	Mr	Holton	Winston		1989608	Sapper 703 RE		Little Horwood
20	19	Detling	Mr	Hopwood	Hervey C Rowan	02/08/1919	903368	Sergeant	500	Maidstone
21	20	Detling	Mr	Jones	Alan John		951462	AC2		Birmingham
22	21	Detling	Mr	Kemble	Charles		1461706	Gunner 268/67		Maidstone
23	22	Detling	Mr	Kennewell	Ernest Victor		1559635	Gunner 265/67		Maidstone
24	23	Detling	Mr	Knowles	Horace Arthur		1989454	Sapper 703 RE		Maidstone
25	24	Detling	Mr	Leder	Louis de Lorne		11191	Sqn Leader		Penton Mewsey
26	25	Detling	Mr	Lee	Donald Harvey	23/03/1918		AC2		
27	42	DoW	Mr	Loham	William H George	05/10/1909	365473	Acting F/Sgt		Chatham
28	26	Detling OB	Mr	Lowe	James Henry		33119	Sqn Leader	500	Maidstone plot 114
29	27	Detling	Mr	Mcdonald	James		639844	AC1		Montrose
30	28	Detling	Mr	Messent	Frederick		812073	Sergeant	500	Maidstone plot 99
31	29	Detling	Mr	Mountste-phen	Arthur Donald		79753	Pilot Officer		Bristol
32	30	Detling OB	Mr	Neale	William		612304	AC2	500	Maidstone
33	31	Detling	Mr	O'Kelly	Ronald	06/04/1919	559631	LAC	53	Plymouth
34	32	Detling	Mr	Oliver	Denis Clare		34109	Sqn Ldr Ops	53	Maidstone plot 91
35	33	Detling	Mr	Pendergrest	James William		6142986	L. Bombardier 268/67		Merton
36	34	Detling	Mr	Price	John Idris	16/07/1911	510925	Corporal		Maidstone plot 102
37	35	Detling	Mr	Richards	William Lindsey		343318	Sergeant Riger		Maidstone plot 101

Ref	Orig Ref	Airfield	Title	Surname	First Names	DoB	Serial	Rank	Squad-ron	Buried
38	36	Detling	Mr	Seager	Cyril Ernest		1888969	Sapper 660 RE		Maidstone
39	43	DoW	Mr	Sims	Michael Anthony		42364	Pilot Officer		Trowbridge
40	37	Detling	Mr	Smith	John S William	14/06/1920	644581	AC2	53	New Kilpatrick 22
41	38	Detling	Mr	Watehous	Leslie Austen		812240	AC1	500	Maidstone plot 94
42	39	Detling	Mr	Wood	Clement Allen		1457301	Sapper 268/67		Maidstone
43		Detling WAF	WAAF	Ablett	Lucy					
44		Detling WAF	WAAF	Abrahams	Sarah		2575804	Signaller		
45		Detling WAF	WAAF	Andrews	Gemma			Signaller		
46		Detling WAF	WAAF	Archer	Karen		6144723			
47		Detling WAF	WAAF	Armitage	Sally		4618175			
48		Detling WAF	WAAF	Armley	Jean					
49		Detling WAF	WAAF	Austin	Elizabeth			LAC1		
50		Detling WAF	WAAF	Banks	Tina		327941	Fueller		
51		Detling WAF	WAAF	Barton	Lisa		6288317	Gunner		
52		Detling WAF	WAAF	Beasdale	Amy					
53		Detling WAF	WAAF	Brooks	Angela		22001161	Medical Corps		
54		Detling WAF	WAAF	Burton	Christina		962311	Balloons		
55		Detling WAF	WAAF	Chartham	Carol					
56		Detling WAF	WAAF	Chivers	Lucy					
57		Detling WAF	WAAF	Edmonds	Rose			Corporal WAAF		
58		Detling WAF	WAAF	Finch	Daphne					
59		Detling WAF	WAAF	Frankham	Lucy					
60		Detling WAF	WAAF	Gascoine	Rita		4197346			
61		Detling WAF	WAAF	Greene	Joyce		864261			
62		Detling WAF	WAAF	Haynes	Josie		875504			
63		Detling WAF	WAAF	Hemmings	Lilian			Warrant Off.		
64		Detling WAF	WAAF	Hewitt	Georgina			Driver		
65		Detling WAF	WAAF	Hinds	Georgina					
66		Detling WAF	WAAF	Holgate	Patricia					
67		Detling WAF	WAAF	Kemble	Jessica		6286701			
68		Detling WAF	WAAF	Kemsley	Carol					
69		Detling WAF	WAAF	Malcolm	Jane		3186611			
70		Detling WAF	WAAF	Mcbride	Jill		2191564			
71		Detling WAF	WAAF	Mccabe	Annie		2189423			
72		Detling WAF	WAAF	Medhurst	Susan			Corporal WAAF		
73		Detling WAF	WAAF	Michales	Beatrice					
74		Detling WAF	WAAF	Patterson	Wendy		788802	Driver		
75		Detling WAF	WAAF	Penrose	Sandra					
76		Detling WAF	WAAF	Price	Joanna			Gunner		
77		Detling WAF	WAAF	Sanders	Josie		1903440	Driver		
78		Detling WAF	WAAF	Sanders	Caroline					
79		Detling WAF	WAAF	Saunders	Abigail					
80		Detling WAF	WAAF	Simmons	Jacky					
81		Detling WAF	WAAF	Studley	Beryl					
82		Detling WAF	WAAF	Ticehurst	Roberta					
83		Detling WAF	WAAF	Watson	Gillian					
84		Detling WAF	WAAF	Weston	Frances					
85		Detling WAF	WAAF	Whitcombe	Emma		2575061	Signaller		
86		Civilian		Merrick	Frank			Visitor		
87		Civilian		Hunt	Jesse			Resident		
88		Civilian		Heron	Walter			Resident		

Church Army Canteen Truck and 165 Spitfire

Detling airfield during Battle of Britain

Friningham Manor - WAAF accommodation

RAF Detling Timeline 13/08/1940

Corporal Joan Pearson awarded GC

Detling Pillbox

Detling airfield bunker

Detling airfield bunker entrance

Remains of the pillbox on Detling Airfield 1940

View looking at Detling Airfield location in 1940

Detling Airfield as it has been developed today

RAF EASTCHURCH (Coastal Command) Isle of Sheppey,
currently H.M. Prison Swaleside (Standford Hill)
Commander Group Captain A. Davison.

Eastchurch Aerodrome (2017)

The Airfield was used as a Royal Navy Air Service Training Field, and Air Armament School and by Coastal Command. Anti-submarines and coastal patrols protected the Thames Estuary – which is why it was a target.

Sq266 Blenheims, Sq1493 Fighter Gunnery School, Sq25 Armament Training School, Sq52 Army Co-operation Wing, Sq263 (moved to Drem), Sq142, Sq35 Blenheims.

Air Attacks

August 13th (Eagle Day) (07:02) - attacked airfield Raid 45 - KG2 Dorniers high level attack, ZG26 BF110s in support, Direct Hit Operations Room, 2 Hangers destroyed, 2 Blenheims of Sq35 destroyed, 1 spitfire damaged. (17:00) Further attack by STG1 and LG1 on route to Rochester and Thames Estuary. **August 15**th - attack by LG1 - 60x JU88s and 40x BF110s, damage, 21 killed. **August 20**th - attack with West Malling, Manston and Eastchurch. **August 28**th - attack with Rochford. **August 31**st - air raid also Croydon, Debden, Biggin Hill, Hornchurch. **September 2**nd - air raid with Detling, Biggin Hill and Hornchurch. **September 4**th - air raid Shorts of Rochester attacked and Vickers at Brooklands.

RAF EASTCHURCH RECORDS AIR28/243	OFFICERS	AIRMEN	CIVILIANS	TOTAL	KILLED
Headquarters Staff					
HQ Staff	30	545	101	676	21
WAAF	3	33		36	
Waiters	0	40		40	
Sub Total	**33**	**618**	**101**	**752**	**21**
Airfield Defences Anti-Aircraft Units 4 machine gun nests					
46th East Surreys	6	55		61	
Searchlight Unit ?? 35th AA	13	57		70	
Royal Engineers					
RE 655	3	55		61	
RE 180	2	33		35	
961st Balloons A Flight	5	203		208	
Observer Corp	29	403		432	
Sub Total	**58**	**806**		**864**	
Total Ground Crew (as per food)					
RAF Squadrons	60	288		348	
No 25 Armaments School					
No 35 Squadron					
No 52 Army Co-operation Squadron					
No 142 Squadron					
No 266 Squadron					
No 1493 Fighter Gunnery School					
Sub Total (estimated)	**60**	**288**		**348**	
Total Airfield Headcount	**151**	**1,712**	**101**	**1,964**	**21**

Examining the damaged plane

Eastchurch bomb damage

Eastchurch pillbox

Relaxing before duty begins

Eastchurch airfield (Luftwaffe photo)

RAF Ground Crew

Eastchurch airfield hangars

RAF Pilots

RAF GOSPORT Group 10 (HMS Sultan) Hampshire
also Fort Grange Field (Stokes Bay)
Commander: Group Captain E.O. Grenfell

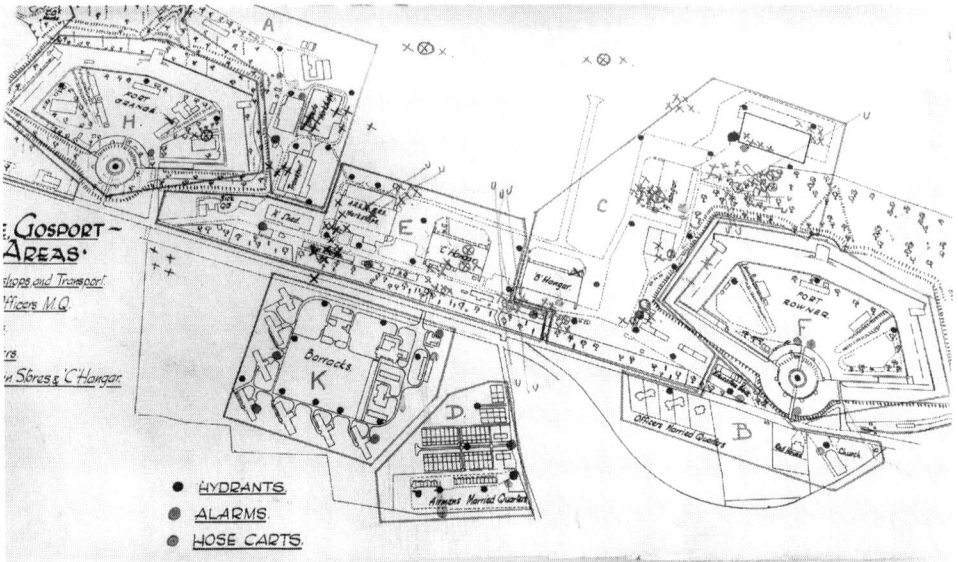

Gosport Airfield Plan

Airfield was 2 units RAF Gosport and Fort Grange Field used for Torpedo Training in Stokes Bay, which was why the airfield was a target to destroy the aircraft before Operation Sea Lion. Squadrons for Torpedoes 460, 461, 462, and 463; Fleet Spotters Sq 420, 421, 422, 423; Air Stores Sq 419; and part of No 12 Training Group Torpedo Development Squadron No 3502.

Air Attacks

August 12th (15:30) KG54 120x JU88, LG1 40x BF109 from Cherbourg then went on to Portland, Middle Wallop and Westhampnett – craters in the runway. **August 16**th - attack leaves very large craters in the runway. **August 18**th - attacked Radar Station at Poling, and Thorney Island – crater damage.

Stokes Bay - Torpedo dropping zone

Swordfish Torpedo bombers, Gosport

RAF GOSPORT RECORDS AIR28/314 & 315	OFFICERS	AIRMEN	CIVILIANS	TOTAL	KILLED
Headquarters Staff					
Commandant Wing-Com					
Admin & Accounts					
Armourers					
Communications -Telephones					
Catering & Mess					
Maintenance					
Operations Room					
Personnel & Records					
Stores & Equipment Sq419					
Transport & Drivers					
Workshops					
Sub Total	40	560	100	700	??
Airfield Defences Anti-Aircraft Units 4 machine gun posts					
"C" Company 8th Hampshires					
No 8 AA Division searchlights					
N0 932 Balloon Squadron					
Sub Total	4	200		204	
RNAS Squadrons					
Torpedo Squadrons (460 to 463)					
Squadron Spotters (420 to 423)					
Torpedo Development Sq 3502					
Sub Total (estimated)	90	432		522	
Total Airfield Headcount	134	1,192	100	1,426	??

Kilkicker AA Gun - Gosport

RAF Bristol Blenheim flies over RAF Gosport

RAF HAWKINGE "Sector D" Near Folkestone, Kent
Wing Commander W.L. Payne (Serial No 05093)

Operations and Armoury

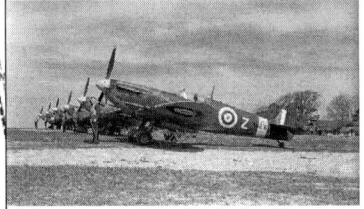

Supermarine Spitfires

RAF Hawkinge Aerodrome

Hawkinge Airfield was in the front line, housed two special Radio Stations for the SOE (Station Y signal receivers from France). Between June & September had a Q Decoy Unit. Squadrons based on site - 32 ,72, 79, 501, 610 (moved to Biggin Hill), 64, 615 (Kenley), 111 (Croydon), 141 (West Malling), Sq245 Hurricane remained. Air Sea Rescue unit from 1944 - Operation Diver.

Air Attacks

August 12th (17:30) Heavy attack by Erpro 210 - 15x JU88s with ZG2 and ZG76 BF109 & BF110 - badly damaged, wrecked the workshops, two married quarters' houses destroyed. 28 Bomb craters in the runway, No3 & No5 Hangar, main stores and clothes store wrecked and destroyed. Two aircraft were damaged and 7 men killed. **August 13**[th] (07:10) slight damage to runway but repaired. August 15th attack by EpGrp210 16x JU87s & BF109s - they attacked Lympne, Shorts factory at Rochester. **September 1**[st] (07:30) air raid 5x ME109s also attacked Detling, Eastchurch and Lympne. Slight damage to runways. **September 2**[nd] Air Raid warning - no attack. **September 5**[th] Also attacked Biggin Hill, Detling, Croydon, North Weald, Lympne and oil tanks.

RAF Hawkinge (© Kent Museum)

Ground crew repair Spitfire

RAF HAWKINGE RECORDS AIR28/345	OFFICERS	AIRMEN	CIVILIANS	TOTAL	KILLED
Headquarters Staff					
Commandant + Control Room	8	58	24	88	
Admin & Accounts	2	9	1	13	
Armourers		228		228	
Communications -Telephones		48		48	
Catering & Mess	2	9		11	
Maintenance		32		32	
Stores & Equipment	2	4	6	10	
Transport & Drivers		42		42	
Workshops		11	1	12	
Sub Total	**14**	**441**	**33**	**488**	**7**
Airfield Defences Anti Aircraft Units					
26th AA Brigade 8 gun pits	4	58		62	
233rd Kent Searchlights					
952nd Sq "C" Flight Balloons					
Royal Engineers (unknown which units)					
Observer Corp					
Sub Total	**18**	**499**	**33**	**550**	**7**
RAF Squadrons					
No 32 Squadron					
No 72 Squadron					
No 79 Squadron					
No 245 Squadron					
No 510 Squadron					
Other Units (estimated)	**50**	**240**		**290**	
Total Airfield Headcount	**86**	**1,238**	**33**	**1,357**	**7**

RAF HORNCHURCH (Call sign LUMBA) "Sector D" HQ
119 Suttons Lane, Hornchurch, Essex, RM12 6RU 01708-862802
Commander: Wing Commander Cecil Bouchier

Hornchurch Aerodrome (1950)

Hornchurch aerial

Four pilots of 611 Squadron RAF

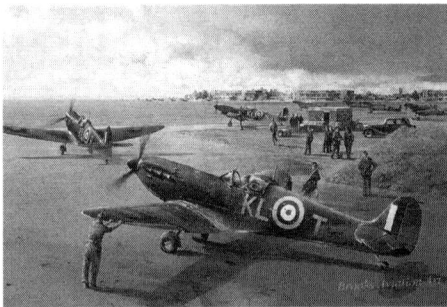

Hornchurch scramble © Brooks Art

The Airfield was the HQ for Sector D - covering the East of England. Squadrons manning the station: Sq41 (EB), and Sq54 (KL) - Spitfires; Sq65 (YT) (East India), Sq74 (ZP) (Trinidad), Sq222 (ZP) (Natal), Sq264 (PS) - Defiants (Madras - moved to Fowlmere), Sq266 (UO) Spitfires from Eastchurch (Rhodesia), Sq600 (BQ) Blenheims (City of London -moved to Northolt), Sq603 (XT) Spitfires (City of Edinburgh) satellite station RAF Rochford. Closed 1962.

Air Attacks

August 13th (Eagle Day) - KG1 HE111s with BF109s dropped bombs and cratered the airfield. **August 24**th - Extensive damage to buildings JU88s DO17s (1 shot down). Air raid attack also North Weald. **August 26**th - KG3 attack 100 bombs dropped. 1 AA gunner killed. Also North Weald and Debden. **August 30**th - Attack aborted by Luftwaffe. **August 31**st (11:30) 30 Dorniers, 100 bombs dropped, slight damage (Airmen's Mess and power cables cut), 3 RAF killed, 11 injured. Air raids also on Croydon, Debden, Biggin Hill, North Weald, Duxford and Eastchurch. **September 2**nd (08:30) attacks also on Biggin Hill, Detling, and Eastchurch. **September 3**rd (09:30) - raid seen off.

Eric Lock 41 Squadron

Hornchurch Control Building

RAF HORNCHURCH RECORDS AIR28/384	OFFICERS	AIRMEN	WAAFs	CIVILIANS	TOTAL	KILLED
Headquarters Staff						
HQ Staff						
WAAF						
Sub Total	30	460	63	30	523	4
Airfield Defences Anti-Aircraft Units 10 gun pits 4 Bofors guns						
Glasgow Highlanders 1 Company						
33rd AA Brigade (Rough Riders)						
28th Essex Searchlights						
910 Squadron Balloon "C"Flight						
Sub Total	26	700	0	0	726	0
Royal Engineers						
unknown						
Sub Total	56	1,160	63	30	1,249	4
RAF Squadrons						
Squadron 41						
Squadron 54						
Squadron 65						
Squadron 74						
Squadron 222						
Squadron 264						
Squadron 266						
Squadron 600						
Squadron 602						
Sub Total Aircrew	90	432	0	0	522	0
Total Airfield Headcount	146	1,592	63	30	1,831	4

RAF KENLEY (Call Sign TOPHAT) "Sector B" Group 11

Bemish Avenue, Kenley, Surrey, CR8 5YG

Commander: Group Captain Victor Beamish (North Weald) and Wing Commander Johnnie Johnson.

Croydon Museum T: 0208-253-1022, E: museum@croydon.gov.uk

Kenley Airfield

Kenley

The Airfield had the following squadrons on station during the air attacks: SQ64 (SH), SQ66 (LZ) - Spitfires, Sq253 (Hyderabad SW - Hurricanes), Sq615 (KW) - Hurricanes, Sq616 (YQ) - Spitfires, joined by Sq350 (Belgium) - Spitfires. The following squadrons were moved: Sq3 (Manston), Sq17 (Debden), Sq229 (Northolt), Sq604(Middle Wallop), Sq85 (Northolt), Sq 66 (moved to Kenley).

Air Attacks

August 13th - attacked by KG2 74x Dorniers & ZG26 60x BF110s, damage.
August 15th - attacked by LG1.
August 16th - attacked with Biggin Hill, Croydon and Northolt by 20x JU87s.
August 18th (13:10) 9x Dornier Do17s with BF109 - attack (100 HE bombs + 24 delayed) - destroyed 3 hangars, Medical Centre, Equipment Store, officers & airmen mess, station HQ, barracks room, transport section (16 vehicles destroyed), craters in the runway and destroyed 4 Hurricanes and 1 Blenheim. Killed 9 aircraftmen and wounded 7 more plus 1 WAAF.
August 26th - attack by KG2 then went on to Biggin Hill, damage.
September 1st (14:30) - 8 bombers + 5 fighters attacked and destroyed 3 huts and 3 houses in Buxton Lane temporary accommodation. Biggin Hill also badly damaged, with North Weald. 1 Army dead and 1 RAF injured.

Luftwaffe He111 brought down - 30.8.1940

Kenley Tower

Flight Lt Brendan Finucane DFC at Kenley

Bombing at Kenley Airfield

RAF KENLEY RECORDS AIR28/419	OFFICERS	AIRMEN	WAAF	CIVILIANS	TOTAL	KILLED
Headquarters Staff						
HQ Staff						
WAAF						
Sub Total	32	482	107	?	621	11
Airfield Defences Anti-Aircraft Units 120 gun pits						
27th AA Brigade						
30th Searchlights						
Squadron Balloon "C"Flight						
Sub Total	36	700	0	0	736	0
Royal Engineers						
unknown						
Sub Total						
RAF Squadrons						
Squadron 64						
Squadron 253						
Squadron 615						
Squadron 616						
Squadron 350 (Belgian)						
Sub Total Aircrew	50	240	0	?	290	0
Total Airfield Headcount	118	1,422	107	?	1,647	11

RAF LYMPNE (HMS Buzzard) "Sector C"
Royal Naval Air Station, Hythe, Kent
Commander A.A. Murray & Group Captain A. Gray.

Lympne Aerodrome

The Airfield was formerly a Royal Naval Air Station and was taken over by the RAF in May 1940, home of Sq601 (County of London moved to Croydon). It concentrated on protecting the English Channel and therefore housed Blenheim bombers SqNos 2, 6, 18, 23, 53 and 59. Douglas Bader flew from there prior to the war. It was near the ports of Folkestone and Dover.

Air Attacks

August 12th (08:00) - attacked by KG2 15x Dorniers DO17. 141 bombs damaged buildings and hangars, 1 aircraftsman killed, 1 Hurricane destroyed. Sq601 moved to Croydon, further raid at 17:40 - Paint store and power cables destroyed.

August 15th (11:30) - attacked by KG76 50x JU88 and SIG1 Me109s - all hangars destroyed with Cinque Ports Flying Club aircraft in them, sick bay, orderly room, accounts office (direct hit). The airfield was evacuated and used for emergency landings only - delayed time bombs dropped.

August 30th (15:54) - attacked by 20 aircraft, destroyed another hangar, hit an air raid shelter, killed 5 pilots and 6 civilians.

September 1st - 3 enemy aircraft attacked, 1 Hurricane damaged, 1 RAF killed (LAC Andrew Antha 571091), also on Biggin Hill, Detling and Eastchurch (September 5th).

Lympne Airfield entrance

Lympne Airfield Control Tower

Destroyed barracks at Lympne

Lympne Air Attack

RAF LYMPNE RECORDS AIR28/509	OFFICERS	AIRMEN	WAAF	CIVILIANS	TOTAL	KILLED
Headquarters Staff						
HQ Staff						
WAAF						
Sub Total						
Airfield Defences Anti-Aircraft Units Machine gun posts only						
26th AA Brigade						
223rd Searchlights						
952 Squadron Balloon 1 Flight						
Sub Total						
Royal Engineers						
unknown						
Sub Total	35	500	65	60	660	7
RAF Squadrons						
Squadron 2						
Squadron 6						
Squadron 18						
Squadron 23						
Squadron 53						
Squadron 59						
Sub Total Aircrew	60	286	?	?	346	?
Total Airfield Headcount	95	786	65	60	1,006	7

RNAS LEE ON SOLENT (HMS Daedalus)

Lee on Solent, Hampshire. PO13 9YA www.solentairport.co.uk

Commander Captain T. Butler

Lee-on-Solent (1928)

Lee on Solent from the air

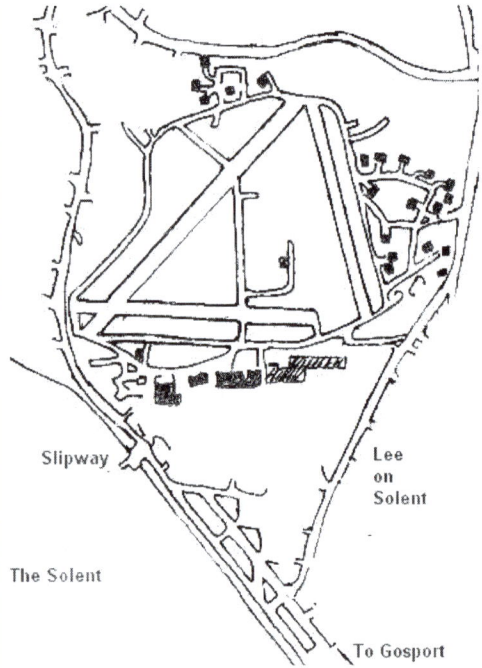

Slipway

The Solent

Lee on Solent

To Gosport

Lee on Solent Airfield plan

Lee on Solent Airfield is in fact two fields. Aircraft and sea plane training on the seafront (Sea Plane Training School under 4/38 School of Navy Co-operation). The airfield was the parent of the following RNAS Stations as well: RNAE Bedhampton Camp, Training Units RNATE - Lympne & Newcastle-under-Lyme, RNAS Lavremry Ferry & Sandbanks. Squadrons on the two Fields - 710 and 765 Walruses, 728 Whirlwinds, 737 Avro Ansons, 753 and 754 Sharks, 770 Gladiators and 772 Tiger Moths. 2 squadrons which were on HMS Arc Royal operated from RAF Lympne and may have been on the airfield Sq Nos 800 and 803. Also on the main field were 2 maintenance units for Aircraft carriers: No3 Barracuda repairs and No1 Avenger repairs. They were targeted as this was a threat to ships being used by the Germans for invasion Operation Sea Lion.

Air Attacks

August 12th - runways cratered, attack on Portsmouth and Radar station, Ventnor, Poling, etc. August 13th (13:10) 5x LG1 JU87s and STG1 BF109s destroyed 42 aircraft on the ground, killed 14. **August 16**th - air raid on Middle Wallop, Brize Norton, Ventnor radar.

Walrus K8556 on the slipway at Lee

Supermarine Walrus (Allan Green)

Lee on Solent slipway

Seaplane at Lee on Solent

RNAS LEE-ON-SOLENT RECORDS AIR28/440	OFFICERS	AIRMEN	WAAF	CIVILIANS	TOTAL	KILLED
Headquarters Staff						
HQ Staff						
WAAF						
Sub Total						
Airfield Defences Anti-Aircraft Units Machine gun posts only						
8th AA Brigade						
223rd Searchlights						
Squadron Balloon 1 Flight						
Sub Total No planes or headcount records. Estimated 14 killed						
Royal Engineers						
unknown						
Sub Total						
RNAS Squadrons - Royal Navy personnel different (needs further investigation to obtain records)						
Squadron 702						
Squadron 712						
Squadron 716						
Squadron 718						
Squadron 2 ACO Flight "A, B, C"		3x 36				
Squadron Float Plane Training		16				
Squadron Communications		10				
Sub Total Aircrew						
Total Airfield Headcount						

RAF MANSTON "Sector D" Ramsgate, Kent CT12 5DF

T: 01843 821940 E: enquiries@spitfiremuseum.org.uk

Commander: Wing Commander A. Jordan and
Squadron Leader G. Manton (5th Sept 1940)

RAF Manston Museum T: 01843 825224

Manston Airfield (Luftwaffe photo)   *Early view of Manston airfield*

RAF Manston was a frontline airfield and was completely destroyed on the 24th of August 1940 after 6 raids on that day. Squadrons were moved and re-housed; for example, WAAFs moved to Ursuline Convent in Westgate-on-Sea. Squadrons on the field: №3 - Hurricanes, №264 - Defiants (moved to Fowlmere), №235 - Blenheims (Filton), №600 - Blenheims (Northolt), №2 Recon Squadron stayed - Wellingtons, №1 Balloon Unit (destroyed August 14th). Inoperable after 24th of August - completely destroyed (unexploded bombs on fields - evacuation needed)

Air Attacks

August 12th (12:50) attack by KG2 15x ME110 + Heinkels - 100 craters on the runways, 2 hangars damaged plus workshops with 2 Blenheims dstroyed 2 civilians killed. Airfield unusable. **August 14th** (11:50) attack by ERG210 80x JU87 and JAG 26 BF109s & BF110s shot down all barrage balloons. 2 hangars destroyed. (Bellman & Bessonneau Hangars) with 3 Blenheims inside, 1 large crater. August 16th (17:45) 8x Me109 hangers & aircraft machine gunned (destroyed 3 Blenhiems and 1 Spitfire), attacked other airfields Biggin Hill, Croydon, Kenley, Northolt and West Malling.
August 18th (16:30) 12x Heinkels HE113s, 2 Spitfires destroyed 1 RAF Killed 15 injured. **August 20th** (15:00) 8x ME109s, 1 Blenheim destroyed other attacks on Eastchurch and West Malling. **August 22nd** (19:00) Squadron Me109, 2x Me110s, 7 bombs, hangar and other airfields attacked on raid.
August 25th (05:30) 6 attacks last at (15:20) by 80x JU88A with escorts; attack leaves airfield unserviceable and was abandoned. (12:50) 7 RAF killed, living quarters damaged + unexploded bomb. Ramsgate attacked and many houses destroyed with 28 civilians killed. This raid destroyed the airfield completely.

Manston No.1 Balloon Unit inflating balloons

Artist's impression of attack on Manston

Bofors in action at Manston

Luftwaffe Me109 shot down

RAF MANSTON RECORDS AIR28/512	OFFICERS	AIRMEN	WAAF	CIVILIANS	TOTAL	KILLED
Headquarters Staff						
HQ Staff						
WAAF						
Sub Total						
Airfield Defences Anti-Aircraft Units 8 gun pits						
58th AA Brigade						
29th Searchlights						
No 1 Squadron Balloon 1 Flight						
Sub Total						
Royal Engineers						
unknown						
Sub Total						
RAF Squadrons						
Squadron 3						
Squadron 2						
Squadron 235						
Squadron 264						
Squadron 600						
Sub Total Aircrew						
Total Airfield Headcount	116	1877	?	?	1,993	38

Note: These National Archive records are not split by unit (total ration list).

RAF MIDDLE WALLOP (Call Sign STARLIGHT)
Group 10 Sector HQ
Middle Wallop, Stockbridge, Hampshire, SO20 8DY
Commander Wing Co D.W Roberts

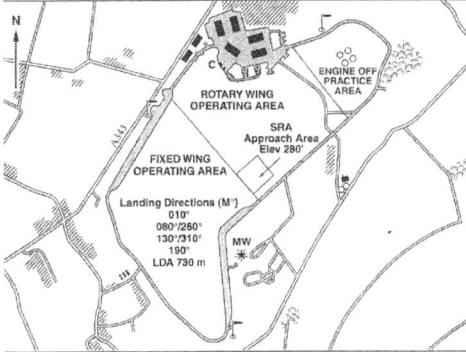

Middle Wallop Airfield map

Middle Wallop Airfield aerial photo

Middle Wallop control tower

Middle Wallop village

The Airfield is now HQ for the Army Flying Corps, and in 1940 was the sector HQ for Group 10 defending the West of England. Squadrons on the field: No15 SFTS Training Oxford, Sq152 (UM) - Spitfires, SQ236 (FA) - Blenheims (moved to Thorney Island), Sq238 (VK) - Hurricanes, (moved to St Eval, August 14th, replaced by No 234), No 601 - Hurricanes (UF) moved to Tangmere, No 604 (NG) - Blenheims, No 609 (PR) - Spitfires, also Signals school located there (Flight Lt Hughes).

Air Raids

August 13th - Attack by STG2 14x JU87 bombed and hit a hangar and hit 609 Squadron's office, killed 3 RAF in 609 Squadron and 3 civilians. **August 14th** - 5 bombs dropped no damage. Air raid - other fields attacked: Manston, Sealand and Cardiff. **August 15th** - LG1 attacked with JU88s, two hangars destroyed, 1 aircraft destroyed and 5 damaged. **August 16th** - other fields attacked Tangemere, Gosport, Lee, Ventnor, Middle Wallop and Brize.

German raid at Middle Wallop 1940

RAF Middle Wallop operations room

Spitfires in formation

No 504 Squadron RAF at Middle Wallop

RAF MIDDLE WALLOP RECORDS AIR28/545	OFFICERS	AIRMEN	WAAF	CIVILIANS	TOTAL	KILLED
Headquarters Staff						
HQ Staff						
WAAF						
Sub Total						
Airfield Defences Anti-Aircraft Units Unknown gun pits						
5th AA Division						
Searchlights						
Squadron Balloon 1 Flight						
Sub Total						
Royal Engineers						
unknown						
Sub Total	35	500	65	60	600	0
RAF Squadrons						
Squadron No 15 SFTS						
Squadron No 152						
Squadron No 236						
Squadron No 238						
Squadron No 601						
Squadron No 604						
Squadron No 609						
RAF Signals School						
Sub Total Aircrew	80	384	?	?	464	?
Total Airfield Headcount	115	884	65	60	1,124	?

RAF NORTH WEALD (Call Sign COWSLIP) Harlow, Essex "Sector E"
Commander: Wing Com H.D. O'Neill (appointed 31st Dec 1939)
then Group Captain Victor Beamish
T: 01992 564200 North Weald Charity 0208-5054555 www.northweald.org

North Weald Airfield 1940   *North Weald Airfield (recent)*

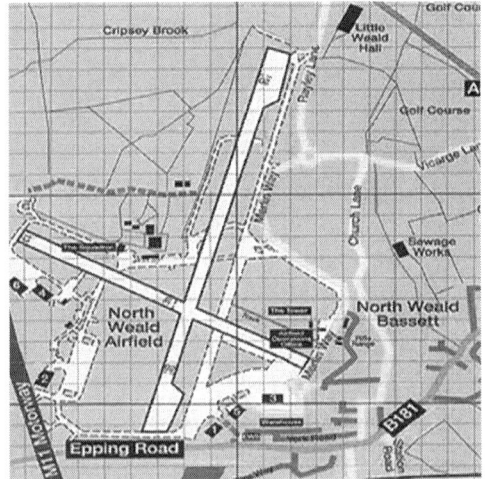

The Airfield had the following squadrons on its field in August 1940, its subsidiary airfield was RAF Stapleford Tawney:
Sq No56 (US) Hurricane Sq Leader A. Pratt; No2 (ZK) ?; No57 ?; Sq No151 (DZ) Hurricane. Sq Leader E.M. Donaldson; No419 Flight. The other squadrons moved to No1 (Northolt), No1 RCAF (Northolt), No46 (Stapleford), No257 (Northolt). No 604 (moved to North Weald 29th Sept).

Air Raids

August 13th (Eagle Day) (05:12) KG2 50x Dorniers Do17, and KG54 Ju88s some damage. **August 22nd** - other airfields attacked Manston.
August 24th (15:40) - 30x Do215 +100x He111 and Me109s. 200 bombs dropped hit and destroyed Officers' Mess, Airman's quarters, killed 9 men from the Essex regiment direct hit on shelter, this air raid also destroyed RAF Manston. A lot of bombs hit the Epping and Ongar Roads.
August 30th - 15x Do17s attacked Biggin Hill and Kenley which were severely damaged as well.
August 31st (10:25) 17x He111 and 22x Me109s air raid on Croydon, Debden, and Hornchurch.
September 3rd 25x Do215s and 50x Me109s attack and destroyed Operations Room and several hangars, 1 Blenheim destroyed, killed 5 and wounded 39.
September 5th Air raid attack on Biggin Hill, Croydon, Detling, and Lympne, oil terminal at Thameshaven.

North Weald Control Tower

Damaged hangar

North Weald Airfield Museum

Type A hangar

RAF NORTH WEALD RECORDS AIR28/603	OFFICERS	AIRMEN	WAAF	CIVILIANS	TOTAL	KILLED
Headquarters Staff						
HQ Staff						
WAAF						
Sub Total						
Airfield Defences Anti-Aircraft Units 15 gun pits						
59th AA Division						
29th Essex Searchlights						
Squadron Balloon 1 Flight						
Royal Engineers						
unknown						
Sub Total						
RAF Squadrons	35	500	65	60	600	9
Squadron No 1						
Squadron No 1 RCAF Canadians						
Squadron No 2						
Squadron No 56						
Squadron No 57						
Squadron No 146						
Squadron No 151						
Squadron No 257						
Squadron No 419						
Sub Total Aircrew	90	432	?	?	512	1
Total Airfield Headcount	125	932	65	60	1,172	10

RAF/RNAS PEMBROKE DOCK

Pembroke Historical Society Dock Museum www.sunderlandtrust.com
Air Cadets Pembroke SA72 6TR
Commander: John (Jock) Evans

Pembroke Dock - plan   *Luftwaffe photo of Pembroke Dock 1940*

Pembroke was originally Paterchurch, a small fishing village, taken over by the Royal Navy. Its main task was Anti Submarine Patrols, but also stored large fuel tanks and oil supplies, as this was the largest natural harbour in the UK for tankers. Squadrons which were on station were 4 squadrons of Sunderland Flying Boats: Sq Nos 10 (Australian), 48, 203, 209, 210 and 228 - long range aircraft. During 1940, eight Dutch Royal Navy seaplanes arrived, Fokker sea planes escaped from Holland. This became Sq Nos 320 and 321 and moved to RAF Carew Cheriton Air Sea Rescue squadrons on the station.

Air Attacks

July 28th - Sunderlands drove off an air attack.

August 19th (15:00) - Sig 1 3x JU88 and Jag27 2x ME109s attacked the oil terminal and set alight 18 large oil tanks. The terminal held over 33 million gallons of oil. The fire lasted for 18 days and injured over 1100 people - a major Fire Oil Depot.

August 23rd - also attacked Cardiff & Swansea.

September 1st (11:00)- attack on the base, but hit many houses in Pembroke and 4 killed. Also hit Temperance Hall, Treymeyrick Street, Park Street, Diamond Street, and some buildings on the base.

Australian airmen on parade in RAF Station

Luftwaffe bombed Pembroke oil tanks

Pembroke - air sea rescue

Sunderland II of No 10 Squadron RNAS

RAF PEMBROKE RECORDS AIR28/628	OFFICERS	AIRMEN	WAAF	CIVILIANS	TOTAL	KILLED
Headquarters Staff						
HQ Staff						
WAAF						
Sub Total						
Airfield Defences Anti Aircraft Units 1 bofors tower + machine guns						
9th AA Division						
Searchlights						
Squadron Balloon 1 Flight						
№ 21 Balloon Store						
Royal Engineers						
unknown						
Sub Total						
RNAS Squadrons	35	500	65	60	660	4
Squadron № 48						
Squadron № 10						
Squadron № 203						
Squadron № 209						
Squadron № 210						
Squadron № 228						
Squadron № 320						
Squadron № 321						
Squadron № 461						
Air Sea Squadron						
Sub Total Aircrew	100	450	?	?	580	?
Total Airfield Headcount	135	980	65	60	1,240	4

RNAS PORTLAND (HMS Sarepta - later HMS Osprey)
with Chain Home Radar Station

Commander: Comdr Admiral Sir William James (Portsmouth area)

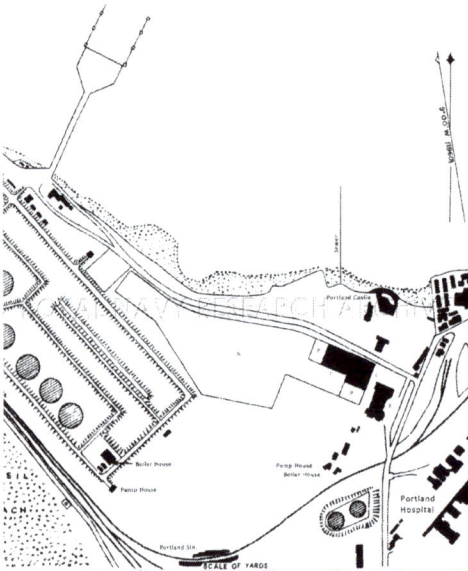

Portland plan

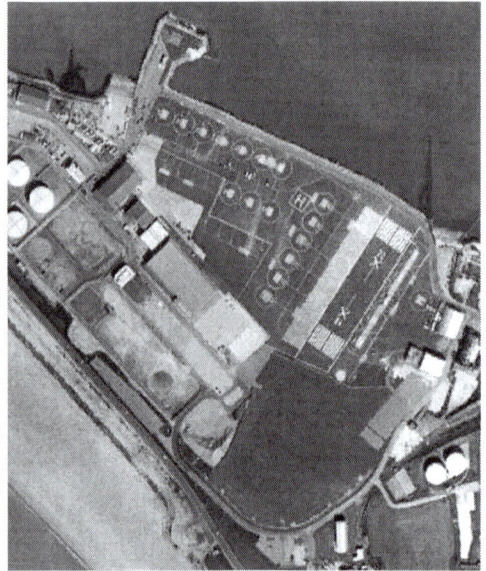

Portland R.N.A.S

This was the Royal Navy Communication Centre which is why it was a target, on the site was also as a chain radar station and a large oil terminal, no squadrons were there until the 1950s. It was used for training however, and was protected by an anti-aircraft ship, HMS Foylebank. It suffered 48 air attacks in 1940. RNAS № 772 Squadron was on the base but moved to Campletown in July 1940 (Sunderlands).

Air Attacks

July 4th - Attack on HMS Foylebank, anti-aircraft ship, in the harbour, lost 176 crew out of 226 by 26x Ju87s. Victoria Cross awarded to Leading Seaman Jack Foreman Mantle.

August 11th - Attack by Kg3 30x BF110 and Kg54, 20x He111 Heinkels.

August 13th (11:40) - Attack by Zer 2 20x B110 and Sig 2 Ju87 on the establishment, hit a lot of buildings and the chain radar station.

August 15th - Attack by Sg87 on Exeter beaten off.

Harbour with Chesil Beach and Lyme Bay

Coaling shed and stores

RNAS Portland Beresford
- old Admiralty Building

Mere oil fuel depot

RNAS PORTLAND RECORDS ADMI/10765	OFFICERS	AIRMEN	WAAF	CIVILIANS	TOTAL	KILLED
Headquarters Staff						
HQ Staff						
WAAF						
Sub Total						
Airfield Defences Anti-Aircraft Units - machine gun posts AA Ship						
8th AA Division						
Searchlights						
Squadron Balloon 1 Flight						
HMS Foylebank						
Sub Total	23	200			223	176
Royal Engineers						
unknown						
Sub Total	35	500	65	60	660	176
RNAS Squadrons						
RNAS Squadron 772						
Air Sea Squadron						
Sub Total Aircrew	20	96	?	?	116	?
Total Airfield Headcount	55	596	65	60	776	176

RAF ROCHFORD (Southend Airport) satellite to Hornchurch
Southend on Sea, Essex, SS2 6YF   Telephone 01702-538500
Commander: Wing Com B.E. Embry (28th Oct 1940)

RAF Rochford (archives)

RAF Rochford (aerial photo 1940)

This airfield was a satellite to RAF Hornchurch. It had a chain radar station on the base and the following squadrons: № 54 Hurricanes, № 74 Blenheims, № 264 Defiants (from Fowlmere posted 29th Oct 1940), № 600 moved to Hornchurch and № 310 to Duxford. № 121 Eagle Squadron (USA arrived in 1941) so did № 71. Chain Home Radar was on site, which is why it was a target.

Air Attacks

August 12th - Attack by KG27 20x Heinkels and Leh1 30x BF110. Destroyed Chain Radar station. **August 26th** - KG2 Dornier shot down. **August 28th** - 2 attacks: first attack KG2 Heinkels HE111 destroyed 27 buildings and second attack left 30 craters in the airfield. **August 30th** - Further attack by 15x HE111, left time bombs with delayed fuses on the airfield, making it inoperable.

Hurricane being serviced

Hurricanes landing

Sqn No 54 pilots in front of Spitfire

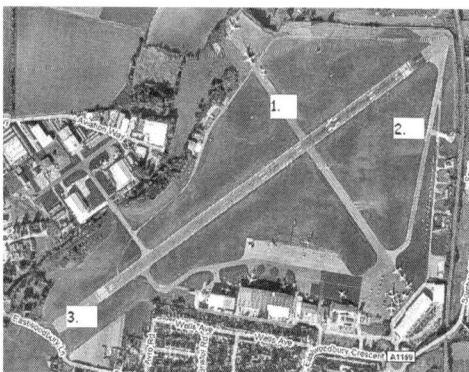

Rochford airfield (current)

Rochford pillbox

RAF Defiants

RAF ROCHFORD RECORDS AIR28/692	OFFICERS	AIRMEN	WAAF	CIVILIANS	TOTAL	KILLED
Headquarters Staff						
HQ Staff						
WAAF						
Sub Total						
Airfield Defences Anti-Aircraft Units - 10 AA units + machine guns						
59th AA Division						
28th Essex Searchlights						
910th Squadron Balloon "B" Flight						
Chain Radar Station						
Sub Total						
Royal Engineers						
unknown						
Sub Total	35	500	65	60	660	?
RAF Squadrons						
Squadron No 54						
Squadron No 74						
Sub Total Aircrew	20	96	0	0	116	?
Total Airfield Headcount	55	596	65	60	776	?

RAF / RNAS ST EVAL (HMS Vulture / Curlew)
St Merryn, Padstow, Cornwall TR8 4HR
Commander link with RAF St Mawgan and RAF St Merryn,
(substitute Airfield RAF Trebelze).
Commander: (RAF St Mawgan) Wing Com Heidi Madden

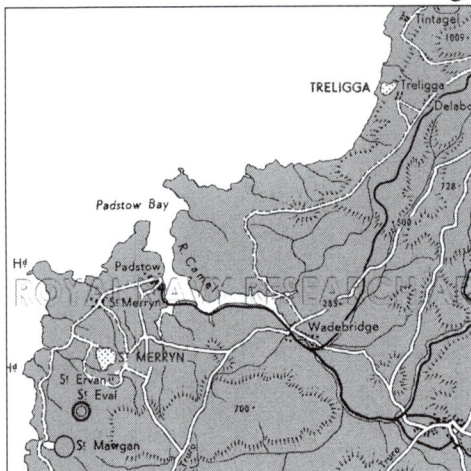

Treligga map

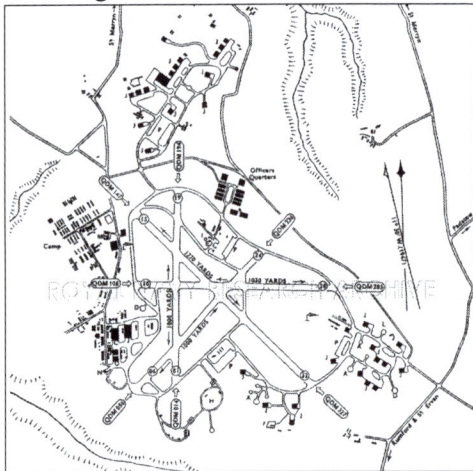

St Merryn airfield plan

This airfield's job was photo reconnaissance, coastal patrols, anti-submarine and shipping patrols, and Air Target Training School Sq № 725. Later other training units arrived on the airfield: № 709 Ground Attack, №s 715 & 736 Air Combat School, № 794 Air Firing School. During the Battle of Britain other squadrons on the field were № 48 - Bristol Beauforts and Avro Ansons, № 217 - Avro Ansons, and from November 1940 № 221 - Wellingtons. Some squadrons moved: № 234 Spitfires to Middle Wallop, № 222 to Hornchurch. There was a Photo Reconnaissance Unit № 1 PRU (Flights A, B, C and D) and №2 Anti Aircraft co-operation Unit. Substitute airfields RAF Trebelze (Ferry Command), RAF St Mawgan and St Merryn.

Air Attacks

July 9th (14:00) a single JU88 dropped 8 bombs causing some damage and was chased by 2 Spitfires. **August 21**st - Attack by 3x JU88s caused damage to 2 hangars and destroyed 2 Blenheims. **August 22**nd - Attack dropped 14 high explosive bombs and 200 incendiaries - did not cause much damage. **August 23**rd - Direct hit on a pyrotechnics store caused a large explosion. **August 26**th - 2 attacks on St Eval at 21:30 and 21:58 hours. **September 30**th (23:00) 5 bombs dropped no damage. **October 3**rd (06:55 & 07:10) - 1 Spitfire and 2 Avros destroyed and 2 hangars damaged. **October 14**th (21:11) 6 high explosive bombs dropped and 20 incendiaries. **January 25**th (19:41) worst raid - hundreds of incendiaries dropped and 21 airmen killed.

RAF St Merryn control tower

Sq 238 at St Eval 1940

RAF St Eval Memorial

RAF St Eval

RAF ST EVAL RECORDS AIR28/733	OFFICERS	AIRMEN	WAAF	CIVILIANS	TOTAL	KILLED
Headquarters Staff						
HQ Staff						
WAAF						
Sub Total						
Airfield Defences Anti-Aircraft Units - machine gun posts						
8th AA Division						
Searchlights						
Squadron Balloon 1 Flight						
Sub Total						
Royal Engineers						
unknown						
Sub Total	35	500	65	60	660	21
RAF Squadrons						
RNAS Squadron 709						
RNAS Squadron 715						
RNAS Squadron 725						
RNAS Squadron 736						
RNAS Squadron 794						
PRU 1						
Squadron No 48						
Squadron No 217						
Squadron No 221						
Sub Total Aircrew	90	432			512	?
Total Airfield Headcount	125	932	65	60	1,112	21

RAF TANGMERE (Call Sign SHORTJACK) Sector A HQ
Chichester, West Sussex, PO20 2ES
Commander: Wing Com D.J.A Boret (later Douglas Bader)
RAF Tangmere Museum

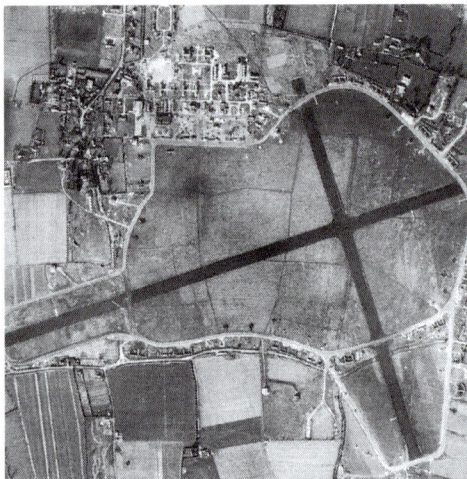

RAF Tangmere airfield 1940   *RAF Merston (satellite of RAF Tangmere)*

The airfield had a subsidiary airfield RAF Westhampnett, and was also the sector HQ for Sector A. It had the following squadrons on the airfield for the Battle of Britain, (all Hurricane squadrons): Sq 43 (FT), Sq 145 (SO), Sq 601 (UF), Sq 607 (AF), Sq 614 moved to Kenley. The Germans' plan was to knock out all sector airfields, which meant that the RAF Dowding system could not function. There was a special squadron of Lysanders - Sq № 161 (Special Duty Squadron) reserved for agents being taken over to France, (see my book on the French Resistance and Special Operations Executive).

Air Attacks

August 13th (Aldertag/Eagle Day) - Attack by Zer26 60x BF110s and KG2 74x Doniers. **August 16**th - Attack started at 13:00 by 50x JU87s from SG2 and Me109s from KG54 - destroyed 3 hangars, Officers Mess, water pumping station, sick bays, 3 workshops. 14 RAF were killed, anti aircraft units on the roof and 6 civilians killed. **August 30**th - Attacks also on Biggin Hill, Oxford and Shoreham.

Tangmere air raid
August 16, 1940

Tangmere control tower

Spitfires being prepared at Merston

Tangmere Aviation Museum

Hurricane parked in a 'blast pen'

RAF TANGMERE RECORDS AIR28/815	OFFICERS	AIRMEN	WAAF	CIVILIANS	TOTAL	KILLED
Headquarters Staff						
HQ Staff						
WAAF						
Sub Total						
Airfield Defences Anti-Aircraft Units - machine gun posts						
8th AA Division						
Searchlights						
Squadron Balloon 1 Flight						
Sub Total						
Royal Engineers						
unknown						
Sub Total	35	500	65	60	660	6
RAF Squadrons						
Squadron 43						
Squadron 145						
Squadron 161						
Squadron 601						
Squadron 607						
Sub Total Aircrew	50	288			338	?
Total Airfield Headcount	85	788	65	60	998	6

RAF THORNEY ISLAND   Havant, Hampshire
Commander: Group Captain T. Langford-Salisbury

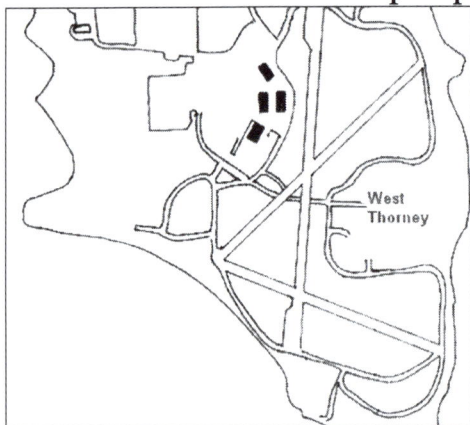

Thorney Island airfield map

Thorney Island airfield - aerial photo

Bristol Beauforts

Observer Group's Blenheim

The airfield was a torpedo development site, had a General Reconnaissance Unit Sq No 3 GRU, and housed the following squadrons in the Battle of Britain for Coastal defence and anti invasion operations:

Squadrons No 235 (moved) and No 236 - Bristol Blenheim; No 58 (moved) and then No 59 - Bristol Blenheims; No 22 - Vickers Wildebeest; No 3 GRU School of General Reconnaissance. The island was taken over by the Royal Artillery, Air Sea Rescue Squadron Training Unit and No 1112 later in 1940.

Air Raids

August 13th (Eagle Day) (13:10) - Small raid 1x JU88, 4 bombs, 1 aircraft hit, no casualties. Attack by a larger raid on the South Coast by Stg77 20x JU87s Junkers, damaged sustained, went onto attack Ventnor and Poling radars amongst other targets. **August 16**[th] (18:14) - 1x JU88 attacked 3 bombs dropped, 2 hangars hit, 4 aircraft damaged, no casualties. **August 18**[th] (14:20) - 25x JU87 6x ME109s 35x HE dropped bombs -2 hangars hit, 3 aircraft hit, 5 civilians wounded. In the same air raid hit RAF Ford, Gosport, and Poling radar. **August 23**[rd] - Air Raid warning 'Red', no attack or bombs dropped, Heinkels driven off.

RAF Rescue and Survival School

Thorney Island Officers Mess

Sqn No.22 sea rescue

No.235 Sqn Beaufighter

RAF THORNEY ISLAND RECORDS AIR28/838 & 844	OFFICERS	AIRMEN	WAAF	CIVILIANS	TOTAL	KILLED
Headquarters Staff						
HQ Staff						
WAAF						
Sub Total	**35**	**500**	**65**	**60**	**660**	**?**
Airfield Defences Anti-Aircraft Units - 8 gun posts						
51st HAA	1	63			64	
76th /218 LAA						
10th Anti-Tank Regiment						
Royal Sussex Regiment	2	82			84	
Searchlights						
Squadron Balloon 1 Flight						
Sub Total						
Royal Engineers						
RE 63rd	1	44			45	
RE 137th	1	54			55	
Sub Total (Non air crew)	**40**	**743**	**65**	**60**	**908**	**?**
RAF Squadrons						
Squadron No 3	1	68			69	
Squadron No 59	32	537			569	
Squadron No 235	10	68			78	
Squadron No 236	30	299			329	
Squadron No 1112	?	?			?	
Sub Total Aircrew	**73**	**939**			**1,012**	**?**
Total Airfield Headcount	**85**	**788**	**65**	**60**	**1,920**	**?**

RAF WEST MALLING (Sector C)

Gibson Drive, Kings Hill, Maidstone, Kent. ME19 4LG

Commandant: Wing Com R.W.K Stevens (2nd July 1940)
then T.B. Prickman (24th July 1940) later Douglas Bader (617 Squadron)
Hawker Typhoon Preservation Group and the West Malling Society

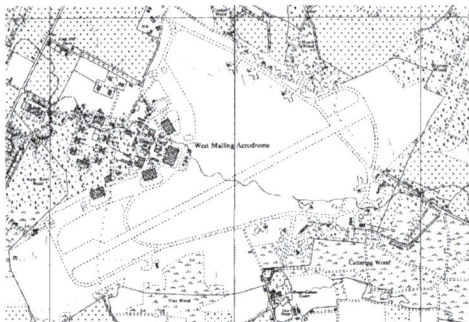

West Malling plan

West Malling Airfield

Douces Manor House (Officers' Mess)

*Blenheim Bomber - West Malling
Home of the Night Fighters*

This airfield was a front-line airfield the following squadrons were on the airfield for the Battle of Britain: Sq №26 Lysanders (used for reconnaissance), №141 Defiants (July 12th - a flight of 9, 6 were destroyed by ME109s in the air), Sq №29 Blenheims (moved to Debden), №32 Hurricane (moved to Biggin Hill), №66 Spitfires (moved to Kenley), the Hurricane and Spitfire squadrons were moved to protect them from the onslaught. The airfield was protected by a Bofors Gun Tower on Green Sand Ridge overlooking the airfield. Officers Mess at Douces Manor. 28th October №66 moved in.

Air Attacks

August 10th (07:30) 1 Heinkel 15 bombs dropped, 2 Lysanders destroyed some damage to runway and workshops, 17 civilians injured, 3 army killed.
August 15th (14:50 &18:20) EPR210 and KG2 attacked Sq 32 on the ground damage to runways. 2 RAF killed, destroyed an ambulance. **August 16th** (13:00) Follow up raid damaged buildings. No casualties. **August 18th** (13:20) Attacked again, damage to new hangar, 3 Lysanders destroyed. **August 21st** Several bombs dropped during the night. **August 24th** - Attack left unexploded bomb on the airfield. **September 3rd** (15:12) - 6 aircraft, 30 bombs, 1 civilian wounded, 20 craters on the runway.

"The Airman" - West Malling

West Malling airfield buildings

West Malling control tower

RAF West Malling memorials

RAF WEST MALLING RECORDS AIR28/907 & 908	OFFICERS	AIRMEN	WAAF	CIVILIANS	TOTAL	KILLED
Headquarters Staff						
HQ Staff						
WAAF						
Sub Total	35	500	65	60	660	?
Airfield Defences Anti-Aircraft Units - 12 gun posts						
147th LAA	1	57			58	
34th LAA	1	37			38	
67th Anti-Tank Regiment	?	?			?	
2nd Battalion 7th Queens Regiment	2	60			62	
30th Searchlights	?	?			?	
961st Squadron Balloon "C" Flight	?	?			?	
Sub Total						
Royal Engineers						
unknown	?	?			?	
Sub Total (Non aircrew)	39	654			818	5
RAF Squadrons						
Squadron № 26						
Squadron № 32						
Squadron № 66						
Squadron № 141	18	305			325	
Squadron № 421	7	83			90	
Sub Total Aircrew	50	532			582	?
Total Airfield Headcount	89	1,186	65	60	1400	5

Chapter 9

Citations Won on Air Raids

With write-ups on each

RAF Citations in 1940

1. Victoria Cross (4th July 1940) Portland Harbour HMS Foylebank - Leading Seaman Jack Foreman Mantle.

2. Military Medal (30th August 1940) RAF Biggin Hill - WAAF Sergeant Elizabeth Mortimer, Sergeant Helen Turner and Corporal Elspeth Henderson. Plus Station Officer Felicity Hanbury Control Room hit.

3. Military Medal (31st May 1940) RAF Detling - WAAF Corporal Pearson, pulled out pilot from burning aircraft.

4. Military Medals (13th August 1940) RAF Detling - Sergeant Mary Youle and Corporal Jessie Robins.

5. Victoria Cross (16th August 1940) Boscombe Down - Pilot Office James Brindley Nicolson.

6. DFC (16th August 1940) Hornchurch, № 74 Squadron - Brian Lane (Sandy).

7. DFC (25th May 1940) Duxford, № 19 Squadron - Adolph Malan.

8. DFC (13th August 1940) Tangmere, № 601 Squadron - Billy Fiske.

9. DFC (6th September 1940) Tangmere, № 1 Squadron - Arthur Clowes (Darky).

10. DFC (21st August 1940) Northolt, № 303 Squadron - Witold Urbanowicz.

11. DSO (30th August 1940) Coltishall - Douglas Bader, combat leadership 22 kills.

12. DFC (24th August 1940) Croydon - Geoffrey Allard, (Sammy), 24 kills.

13. DFC (25th August 1940) Exeter, № 213 - Derek Atkinson, 12 kills.

14. DSO & DFC (24th August 1940) Debden, № 9 - John Braham, 29 kills.

15. DFC (24th August 1940) Northolt, № 600 - Archie D.M.Boyd, 29 kills.

16. DFC (13th August 1940) Hornchurch, № 54 - Flight Lt A.C. Deere.

17. DFC (13th August 1940) Hornchurch, № 74 - Squad Ldr D.G. Malan.

18. DFC (13th August 1940) Hornchurch, № 65 - Sergeant Franklin.

Write-ups on RAF Medal Recipients

1. VC – Leading Seaman Jack Foreman Mantle

4th July 1940 Portland Harbour - HMS Foylebank was protecting the Naval Base and Air Station together with the Oil Depot at Mere Island- the ship had anti-aircraft guns and was manned by 226 naval personnel. The ship was attacked by 20x JU87 Stukas and sank. Jack Foreman Mantle manned his machine gun and shot down several planes, before being wounded by a bomb in his leg. He carried on. He is buried in the Royal Naval Churchyard at Portland Bill with 175 of his shipmates who also lost their lives on that day.

Jack Foreman Mantle

Press Announcement

"On 3rd September 1940 it was announced that the posthumous award of a VC had been made to Leading Seaman Jack Foreman Mantle, of HMS Foylebank which ... was attacked by an enemy aircraft on the 4th of July, 1940. Early in the action his left leg was shattered by a bomb, but he stood fast at his gun and went on firing with hand-gear only; for the ship's electric power had failed. Almost at once he was wounded again in many places. Between his bursts of fire he had time to reflect on the grievous injuries of which he was soon to die; but his great courage bore him up till the end of the fight, when he fell by the gun he had so valiantly served."

2. Military Medals – Elizabeth Mortimer, Helen Turner, Elspeth Henderson and Station Officer Felicity Hanbury (Peake).

During the air raid at Biggin Hill, Elspeth Henderson helped dig out personnel entombed when a bomb hit an air raid shelter where 39 were killed and also manned communication with Uxbridge in the Ops Room during the air raid. Helen Turner manned her post on the telephone exchange during the air raid, she was not aware that she had been leaning against an unexploded bomb. Elizabeth Mortimer also manned her post during the air raid and showed courage and leadership throughout.

(L-R) Elizabeth Mortimer, Elspeth Henderson and Helen Turner

On the same day Station Officer Felicity Hanbury was also awarded the Military Medal and MBE for her leadership of her 200 WAAFs in her charge. She later married (name Peake) and became an Air Commodore.

Felicity Hanbury (Peake)

3. Military Medal – 31st May 1940 (RAF Detling) WAAF Corporal Daphne Pearson - pulled out crew from burning aircraft.

At 01:15 hrs an Avro Anson of 500 Squadron at RAF Detling crashed. Daphne was a WAAF Medical orderly attended, one of the bombs in the Avro exploded killing the wireless operator and injuring the pilot and the other two crewmen. The explosion was very loud and Daphne rushed to the crash site when she heard it. She climbed into the wreckage of the burning Anson, revived the stunned Flying Officer David Bond, releasing his parachute harness, and helped him get clear. Then she dragged him 27 metres away from the burning aircraft and administered first aid. The pilot said the aircraft was still full of fuel and bombs and told her to go, when another bomb ex-

Daphne Pearson

ploded Daphne shielded the pilot from the blast. She stayed with the pilot until the stretcher parties arrived and then hurried back to find the other crew member who was dead, the two others had got out and she tended their wounds until 3.00 am.

4. Military Medals – 13th August 1940 (RAF Detling) WAAF Corporal Josephine Maude Robbins and Sergeant Mary Youle.

During the large air raid, both stayed at their posts in the telephone exchange that was hit, and the control room that was hit.

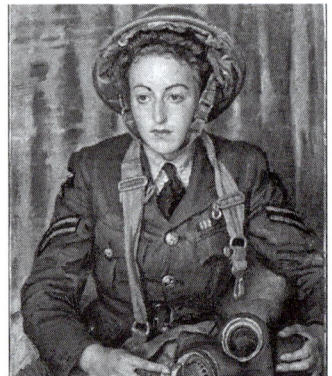

Corporal J M Robins, MM, WAAF

5. Victoria Cross (16th August 1940): Boscombe Down – Pilot Officer James Brindley Nicolson.

Service No 39329 Flight Lieutenant with Sq No.249 that moved to Hornchurch. He was awarded the Victoria Cross on the 16th of August. Above Southampton, from Boscombe Down, his aircraft was hit with cannon fire by four shells, which wounded him and set the Hurricane on fire in the gravity tank. With the cockpit on fire he attacked an BF110 and shot it down, he had severe burns on his legs arms and neck and then he bailed out.

PO James Brindley Nicolson

Victoria Crosses Won in 1940
(Besides The Battle of Britain)

1. VC (12th May 1940) Thomas Gray, RAF № 12 – Albert Canal, Belgium.
2. VC (12th May 1940) Donald Garland, RAF № 12 – Lanakin, Belgium.
3. VC (15th-16th May 1940) 2nd Lt Richard Annand, Durham Light Infantry – River Dyle, Belgium.
4. VC (17th-24th May 1940) Christopher Furness, Welsh Guards – Arras, France.
5. VC (21st May 1940) Harry Nichols, Grenadier Guards – River Escaut, Belgium.
6. VC (21st May 1940) George Gristock, Royal Norfolk Regiment – River Escaut, Belgium.
7. VC (31st May-1st June 1940) Harold Ervine Andrews, East Lancashire Regiment – Dunkirk, France.
8. VC (12th August 1940) Roderick Learoyd, RAF № 49 Squadron – Dortmund Canal, Germany.
9. VC (15th September 1940) John Hannah, RAF № 83 Squadron – Antwerp, Belgium.

Victoria Cross Actions 1940

1. 12th May 1940 - Sergeant Thomas Gray VC - RAF Squadron No.12.

2. 12th May 1940 - Flying Officer Donald Garland RAF Squadron No.12. Both men were in the same aircraft. Garland the pilot and Gray the observer. They were the leading aircraft of five in the formation (Fairey Battles) to attack and destroy a bridge over the Albert Canal in Belgium to stop the German advance. The bridge was heavily protected by aircraft and machine guns and had to be destroyed at all costs. They destroyed the bridge and another bridge at Veldwezelt. Only one aircraft returned, their aircraft was shot down in the village of Lanaken, both died in hospital in Maastricht.

Thomas Gray VC

Donald Garland VC

3. 15th-16th May 1940 - 2nd Lt Richard Annand VC - **Durham Light Infantry.** His platoon was on the south side of the bridge on the River Dyle; he beat off a strong attack. Later at 11:00 a second strong attack, Lt Annand with the ammunition running out, charged the bridge and with grenades, killed 20 Germans with hand grenades, and damaged the bridge. His platoon stayed and later attacked the Germans again before withdrawing his platoon as ordered. However he then went back to retrieve his wounded batman.

Richard Annand VC

4. 17th-24th May 1940 - Lt Christopher Furness VC -1st **Battalion Welsh Guards.** Commanded the Carrier Platoon, garrisoned in Arras, ordered to cover the withdrawal of the garrison to Douai in charge of 40 vehicles. The enemy were advancing along the road. Lt Furness decided to attack. He reached the enemy position under heavy fire and when he had destroyed all the light tanks and carriers and their crews, he engaged them in hand to hand combat until he was killed.

Christopher Furness VC

5. 21st May 1940 - Lance Corporal Harry Nicholls VC - 3rd Battalion Grenadier Guards. On the 21st of May near the River Escaut in the village of Esquelmes (North of Tournai), Lance Corporal Nichols suffering from shrapnel wounds in his arm, continued to lead his section in a counter attack against overwhelming German opposition. He advanced over a ridge and when the position became critical, he rushed forward, putting three machine guns out of action. He then attacked massed enemy infantry until his ammunition ran out and he was taken prisoner.

Harry Nicolls VC

6. 21st May 1940 - Company Sergeant Major George Gristock VC - 2nd Battalion Royal Norfolk Regiment. On the 21st of May near the River Escaut (south of Tournai) Gristock organised a party of 18 riflemen to fill the breach in the right flank of a defence line where the Germans had broken through. With one man, and being wounded in the leg, he reached a good firing position and took out a German machine gun, killing the crew of 4 and then inflicting heavy casualties on the rest. He crawled back to his position and waited for his battalion with its men. He later died of his wounds.

George Gristock VC

7. 31st May to 1st June 1940 - Captain Marcus Ervine-Andrews VC - 1st Battalion East Lancashire Regiment. During the later stages at Dunkirk on the night of the 31st of May, the company commanded by Captain Ervine-Andrews had been ordered to defend 1000 yards of territory on the perimeter. Outnumbered, attacked the Germans across the Canal de Berges, with some men. The Captain rushed forward to a barn, and from the roof shot 17 Germans with his rifle and many more with Bren guns. When the barn was alight he sent the wounded to the rear and led the remaining 8 men back (9 had been killed). Once back to their positions they continued the defence of his line. They were then evacuated later from the beaches. He died in 1995 and lived in Gorran in Cornwall.

Marcus Ervine-Andrews VC

8. 12th August 1940 - **Flight Lieutenant Roderick Learoyd VC - RAF Squadron No.83** (Handley Page Hampden Bombers). Squadrons No.83 and No.49 were ordered to bomb and destroy the old aqueduct carrying the canal over the River Ems, north of Munster. Learoyd was pilot of No P4403 Hampden bomber. He had a crew of 3: Pilot Officer John Lewis (Observer), Sergeant Walter Ellis (Wireless Operator) and Leading Aircraftman William Rich (Gunner). Despite being badly damaged by a flak barrage, he dropped his bombs and destroyed the aqueduct, he then managed to fly his aircraft back to England. He was promoted to Wing Commander in 1958. He died in 1996 in Rustlington, West Sussex.

Roderick Learoyd VC

9. 15th September 1940 - **Sergeant John Hannah VC - RAF Squadron 83 - Handley Page Bombers.** On September 15th the squadron attacked barges in the harbour at Antwerp. Sergeant Hannah was the wireless operator/air gunner. The serial number of aircraft was P1355. The aircraft was subjected to intense anti-aircraft fire, starting a fire which spread quickly. The rear gunner and navigator had to bail out. Hannah fought the fire on his own which he put out, but sustained terrible burns. This allowed the pilot to fly the badly damaged aircraft back to England.

John Hannah VC

Chapter 10
War Cabinet & RAF Structure
The Main Events of 1940

Following the resignation of Chamberlain on the 9th May 1940, Winston Churchill re-organised a War Cabinet with a coalition of all political parties and talents – skills to defend Britain. Labour joined the coalition on the 11th May 1940, endorsed by Parliament on 13th May 1940. The following people were appointed to the War Cabinet in the national interest:

Winston Churchill *Archibald Sinclair* *Charles Portal* *Hugh Dowding* *Cyril Newall*

NAME	POSITION	PARTY
Winston Churchill	Prime Minister	Conservative
Clement Attlee	Deputy Prime Minister	Labour
Neville Chamberlain	President of Council	Conservative
Viscount Halifax	Foreign Secretary	Conservative
Arthur Greenwood	Minister without Portfolio	Labour
Lord Beaverbrook	Minister War Production & Air	Conservative
Sir John Anderson	Lord President	National
Sir Kingsley Wood	Chancellor of the Exchequer	Conservative
Ernest Bevan	Minister of Labour & National Service	Labour
Herbert Morrison	Home Secretary	Labour
The Lord Moyne	Agriculture & Foods	Conservative
Sir Archibald Sinclair	Minister for Air	Liberal
Hugh Dalton	Minister of Economic Warfare	Labour
The Lord Woolton	Minister for Food	Conservative
Duff Cooper	Minister of Information	Conservative
Ronald Cross	Minister for Shipping	Conservative
Herbert Morrison	Minister for Supply	Labour
Sir Henry Page	Secretary of State for War	Conservative
Sir Donald Somerville	Attorney General	Conservative

Air Ministry and RAF Structure

The Air Ministry under Sir Archibald Sinclair, looked after supply and the structure and Organisation of the RAF at Home and Overseas. The RAF Headquarters was based at RAF High Wycombe where it is now on the Chilterns near Walters Ash. Marshall of the Royal Air Force, Sir Cyril Newall was in post until the 25th October 1940, after the Battle of Britain, and was replaced by Sir Charles Portall. He was Air Vice Marshall commander of RAF Bomber Command based at RAF Uxbridge, and was replaced in October by Air Vice Marshall Arthur Harris. Air Vice Marshall Sir Hugh Dowding was commander of RAF Fighter Command HQ based at Bentley Manor, Stanmore.

Air Council Meeting

War Ministry Building

Map Room, Cabinet War Rooms

RAF High Wycombe

We are just making comments here on some of the establishment buildings that were bombed during the Battle of Britain following the main Luftwaffe assault on the RAF airfields in particular the Houses of Parliament and Buckingham Palace.

Houses of Parliament – attacked 14 times starting on the 26th September 1940 and the last attack being between the 10th and 11th May 1941, where the Luftwaffe tried to destroy it. September 26th – hit the Old Palace Yard, St Stephen Porch and south window + statue of Richard the Lion Heart, on the 8th of December the Luftwaffe destroyed the cloisters and on May 14th and 15th there was a lot of damage with 12 direct hits.

Buckingham Palace Attacks – the Palace was attacked nine times, most of the War. The King and Queen resided at Windsor Castle for safety. The first attack was on the 11th September – five bombs were dropped and they destroyed the Palace Chapel and the Palace Quadrangle. The second attack was on the 13th September and left a large crater by the Palace Main Gates. On the 15th September Sgt Ray Holmes of 504 squadron rammed a Dornier DO17 that was making a bombing run attack on the Palace. It crashed at the junction of Buckingham Palace Road. Sgt Holmes landed safely in a garden. There were attacks on the Palace up until 1941.

Chapter 11

Museums and Memorials

1. **RAF Museum Hendon** Graham Way, Hendon, London, NW9 5LL
   Tel: 0208-205-2266.

2. **RAF Museum Cosford** Shifnal, Shropshire, TF11 8UP, Tel: 01902-376200.

3. **RAF Biggin Hill Memorial Air Show** TN16 3BN Tel: 01959-578500, 01959-422414
   (Spitfire Museum).

4. **RAF Croydon Airport Museum** Purley Way, Croydon, CR0 OX2 Tel: 0208-680-5878.

5. **RAF Hornchurch Society** 119 Suttons Way, Hornchurch, Essex, RM12 6KO,
   Tel: 01708-862802.

6. **RAF Kenley, Museum of Croydon** Tel: 0208-253-1022 E: museum@croydon.gov.uk.

7. **RAF Manston Spitfire Museum** CT12 5DF Tel: 01843-821940
   E: enquiries@spitfiremuseum.org.uk.

8. **RAF North Weald Society** E: www.northweald.org Tel: 01992-564200 or
   0208-505-4555.

9. **RAF Pembroke Dock** Jack Evans E: www.sunderlandtrust.com.

10. **RAF Rochford** Southend-on-Sea Airport, SS2 6YF, Tel: 01702-538500.

11. **RAF Tangmere Museum** Nr Chicester, W. Sussex, PO20 2ES, Tel: 01243-790090.

12. **RAF Radar Museum** Norfolk, Tel: 01692-631485 E: curator@radarmuseum.co.uk,
    Doug Rob 63330912 Spitfire Museum Tel: 01959-576767.

13. **Allied Air Forces Memorial & Museum** Elvington, York, YO41 4AU,
    Tel: 01904-608595.

14. **Fleet Air Arm Museum** RNAS Yeolvilton, Ilchester, Somerset, BA22 8HT,
    Tel: 01935-840565.

Biggin Hill Memorial Museum

Biggin Hill Memorial Museum

RAF Museum Hendon

RAF - Hendon Museum

Trusts and Societies

1. **RAF West Malling** Hawker Typhoon Preservation Society.

2. **WAAF Association** Secretary Marian Cope Tel: 01472-232986
    E: waafsecretary@gmail.com.

3. **Battle of Britain Historical Society Ltd** Calais View, Fairlight, East Sussex, TN35 4BP
    - John Pulfer Tel: 01424-814866 E: johnatbobhs@gmail.com.

4. **RAF Historical Records Branch** West End Road, Ruislip, Middlesex, HA4 6NG
    Tel: 0208-833-8175.

5. **Deputy Director of Defence RAF** Shrivenham Tel: 01793-314847
    E: enquiries.dds@da.mod.uk.

6. **Luftwaffe Historical Association** www.volksbund.de.

7. **Fleet Air Arm Association** 4 St James House, London, SW1Y 4JU
    Tel: 0207-930-7722 Navy& Army.

8. **Airfield Research Group** 8 Renhold Road, Wilden, Bedford, MK44 2QA.
    Tel: 01234-771452, www.airfieldresearchgroup.org.uk.

9. **Airfields of Britain Conservation Trust** Suite 225, 2 West Regent Street, Glasgow, G2
    1RN Tel: 0141-206-3660, www.abct.org.uk Ken Bannerman.

10. **RAF Benevolent Fund** 67 Portland Place, London, N18 1AR. Tel: 0207-307- 3348,
    www.rafbf.org.

11. **Lysander Pilots Association** Tom Petch, www.saltfilm.com, Tel: 0207-637-7885 or
    07775-565992.

12. **RAF №53 Sq. Association** Peter Lewis, 46 Bagley Wood Road, Kennington, Oxford,
    OX1 5LY. Tel: 01865-739984.

13. **Air Sea Rescue Sections Club** John Parsons, 22 Paddockhurst Rd, Crawley,
    RH11 8ER. Tel: 01293-52971.

14. **Air Transport Auxilliary** John Webster, 17 Glenister Rd, Chesham. HP5 2AX.
    Tel: 01494-771322.

15. **Balloon Barrage Club** Peter Grawood, Roc Cottage, Trellech Road, Trellech,
    NP25 4AF. Tel: 01600-860376.

16. **Battle of Britain Fighter Assoc.** Group Capt Patrick Tootal, Tel: 01732-870809
    E: battleofbritain@btinternet.com.

17. **Friends of the RAF Museum** Hendon. NW9 5LL. Tel: 0208-205-2266.

18. **Friends of RNAS Yeolvilton** R. Cabble, 3 Axe Valley Close, Mosterton, Beaminster,
    DT8 3JE. Tel: 01308-868569

19. **Hawker Hurricane Society** Iain Arnold, 69 Caswell Close, Farnborough, Hants.
    GU14 8TD. Tel 01252-541317.

20. **RAF Historical Society** Go Capt Dearman, 1 Park Close, Middleton Stoney, Oxon.
    OX6 8ST. Tel: 01869-343327 E: kdearman@compuserve.com

21. **RAF Lodge of Freemasons** Sq Ldr Armstrong, 1 Moorhen Way, Buckingham,
    MK18 1GN, E: lagana1@ntlworld.com.

22. **Royal Observer Corps Museum Trust** Neville Cullingford, 8 Roselands Close, Fair
    Oak, Hants. SO50 8GN. Tel: 023-8009-3823 E: xrocmunc@hants.gov.uk.

Chapter 12

Conclusions

Great Britain was not prepared following the defeat at Dunkirk, it was out-gunned and ill prepared. The War Cabinet was fighting for survival and we were very lucky. Aircraft production was increased and re-supplied the RAF. The Hurricane and Spitfire were better aircraft and faster and the kill rate was higher than the Luftwaffe. Chain Radar and the Dowding system helped identify targets quickly. The Luftwaffe fighter's ranges were limited and so the RAF shooting was easier on the bombers. The main question was - why did Hitler call off the attack and cancel Operation Sea Lion? The answer may lie with the arresting of the German agents who were then turned and were probably feeding Hitler with false information on the continued strength of the RAF. (This will need further work.)

Conclusions in Detail

Why the invasion was postponed and called off:

- Abwehr German agents were persuaded by MI5 to work (other than being hung) with the Allies to feed information that the RAF had plenty of fighter cover and had not been defeated.

- Aircraft production was high under Lord Beaverbrook and increased to over 450 per month, rather than the estimated 150 by the Luftwaffe in Report Blue (Blue by Intelligence Officer Schmidt).

- Bletchey Park had broken the German Enigma codes (Naval codes) and monitored radio traffic, identified German Agent's names (passed on to MI5) and was continuously monitoring German signals (and the Germans did not know).

- A lot of planes were lost by the RAF but not pilots, Air Sea Rescue picked them, the training programme of the RAF was speeded up and this helped reinforce the RAF. The Luftwaffe lost many planes and pilots.

- German Luftwaffe Intelligence was poor and gave false information that the RAF had been defeated. This was supported by German Agent misinformation and thus persuaded Hitler that Operation Sea Lion had to be cancelled.

- The RAF maintenance crews were efficient and repaired runways within 24 hours and the organisation of repairing aircraft was very good, which meant that airfields were operational very quickly.

- Aircraft production was higher - 496 produced in August - which was higher than the losses.

- The Knickebein system, "Headache", was compromised by the RAF Research establishment and code named "Aspirin". Counter measures set up in Anson bombers, allowed the RAF to anticipate and prepare in advance for raids.

- RAF Pilots flew 5-6 sorties per day, and had rest periods, the Luftwaffe pilots only few 1 mission per day, because of the distance and were expected to carry out other duties when they landed, therefore had no time to relax.

- RAF Fighter training was short and intensive, which meant that pilots knew what to do when they arrive at an airfield.

- RAF Aces were posted to airfields and spread out to encourage younger pilot's morale and spread experience which helped the younger pilots.

- German aircraft had to be accompanied (Stukas in particular) with ME109s fighters which tied up resources. The RAF were aware of this and planned their tactics accordingly.

- The bombing of London was a mistake as the RAF were left alone to re-organise.

- RAF Big Wings defeated the Luftwaffe and night fighter's equipment shot down a lot of German aircraft.

Other Books

- 6th British Airborne Landing operations - Eastern Flank.
- Sword Beach operations - 3rd British Division.
- Juno Beach operations - 3rd Canadian Division.
- Gold Beach-operations - 50th British - Allied Division.
- Omaha Beach operations - 1st and 29th US Divisions and 2nd Ranger Battalion.
- Utah Beach Operations - 4th and 90th US Division.
- US 101st Airborne - Western Flank - Sainte-Marie-Mont - Carentan.
- US 82nd Airborne - Western Flank - Sainte-Mere-Eglise.
- French Resistance and Special Operations Executive.
- British & Canadian Beaches (for 75th Anniversary).
- United States Beaches (for 75th Anniversary).

All available from the website
http://www.dday-wardiaries.co.uk